I expected a how-to manual. I got a primer in how to be counter-culturally Christian in these strange days after the deterioration of Christendom. This is the best of pastoral theology: wise at discerning the times, gentle in its recommendations for the care of souls, incendiary as it fires the pastoral vocation all over again. Reading *Funerals* will remind you why you wanted to be a pastor in the first place.

—Jason Byassee,
Butler Chair in Homiletics and
Biblical Interpretation,
The Vancouver School of Theology;
author of *Surprised by Jesus Again*

If any book deserved to be a bestseller, this mini-masterpiece is the one. Who would have thought something titled *Funerals* could be so good? Perry teaches us not only about funerals but about the entirety of Christian dying and living. Pastorally wise, theologically sane, and beautifully written, this book should be *Christianity Today*'s book of the year.

—Matthew Levering,
James N. and Mary D. Perry Jr.
Chair of Theology,
Mundelein Seminary;
author of *Dying and the Virtues*

Opening this book is like walking through a narrow door into a banquet hall. *Funerals* is not a "how to" book but a rich table of theology, history, biblical and practical methods in caring for souls. The writing is compelling and engaging. A rare and much needed book for these days and the future. A must for all pastors.

—Jo Anne Lyon,
general superintendent emerita,
The Wesleyan Church

Funerals

For the Care of Souls

LEXHAM MINISTRY GUIDES

Funerals

For the Care of Souls

TIM PERRY

General Editor
Harold L. Senkbeil

LEXHAM PRESS

Funerals: For the Care of Souls
Lexham Ministry Guides, edited by Harold L. Senkbeil

Copyright 2021 Tim Perry

Lexham Press, 1313 Commercial St., Bellingham, WA 98225
LexhamPress.com

Unless otherwise noted, all Scripture quotations are from the
ESV® *Bible* (*The Holy Bible, English Standard Version*®), copyright
© 2001 by Crossway Bibles, a publishing ministry of Good News
Publishers. Used by permission. All rights reserved.

Print ISBN 9781683594734
Digital ISBN9781683594741
Library of Congress Control Number 2020950424

Lexham Editorial: Todd Hains, David Bomar, Karen Engle,
    Kelsey Matthews, Abigail Salinger
Cover Design: Joshua Hunt
Interior Design: Abigail Stocker
Typesetting: Fanny Palacios

*For Gerry Lougheed Jr. and Geoffrey Lougheed
with deep thanks.*

Contents

Series Preface

WHAT'S OLD IS NEW AGAIN.

The church in ages past has focused her mission through every changing era on one unchanging, Spirit-given task: the care of souls in Jesus' name. Christian clergy in every generation have devoted themselves to bringing Christ's gifts of forgiveness, life, and salvation to people by first bringing them to faith and then keeping them in the faith all life long.

These people—these blood-bought souls—are cared for just as a doctor cares for bodies. The first step is carefully observing the symptoms of distress, then diagnosing the ailment behind these symptoms. Only after careful observation and informed diagnosis can a physician of souls proceed—treating not the symptoms, but the underlying disease.

Attention and intention are essential for quality pastoral care. Pastors first attentively listen with Christ's ears and then intentionally speak with Christ's mouth. Soul care is a ministry of the Word; it is rooted in the conviction that God's word is efficacious—it does what it says (Isa 55:10–11).

This careful, care-filled pastoral work is more art than science. It's the practical wisdom of theology, rooted in focused study of God's word and informed by the example of generations past. It's an aptitude more than a skillset, developed through years of ministry experience and ongoing conversation with colleagues.

The challenges of our turbulent era are driving conscientious evangelists and pastors to return to the soul care tradition to find effective tools for contemporary ministry. (I describe this in depth in my book *The Care of Souls: Cultivating a Pastor's Heart*.) It's this collegial conversation that each author in this series engages—speaking from their own knowledge and experience. We want to learn from each other's insights to enrich the soul care tradition. How can we best address contemporary challenges with the timeless treasures of the Word of God?

In the Lexham Ministry Guides you will meet new colleagues to enlarge and enrich your unique ministry to better serve the Savior's sheep and lambs with confidence. These men and women are in touch with people in different subcultures and settings, where they are daily engaged in learning the practical wisdom of the care of souls in real-life ministry settings just like yours. They will share their own personal insights and approaches to one of the myriad aspects of contemporary ministry.

Though their methods vary, they flow from one common conviction: all pastoral work is rooted in a pastoral habitus, or disposition. What every pastor does day after day is an expression of who the pastor is as a servant of Christ and a steward of God's mysteries (1 Cor 4:1).

Although the authors may come from theological traditions different than yours, you will find a wealth of strategies and tactics for practical ministry you can apply, informed by your own confession of the faith once delivered to the saints (Jude 1:3).

Our Lord doesn't call us to success, as if the results were up to us: "Neither he who plants nor he who waters is anything, but only God who gives the growth" (1 Cor 3:7). No, our Lord asks us to be faithful laborers in the service of souls he has purchased with his own blood (Acts 20:28).

Nor does our Lord expect us to have all the answers: "I will give you a mouth and wisdom" (Luke 21:15). Jesus, the eternal Word of the Father, is the Answer who gives us words when we need them to give to our neighbors when they need them. After all, Jesus sees deeper into our hearts than we do; he knows what we need. He is the Wisdom of God in every generation (1 Cor 1:24).

But wisdom takes time. The Lord our God creates, redeems, and sanctifies merely by his words. He could give us success and answers now, but he usually doesn't. We learn over time through challenges and frustrations—even Jesus grew over time (Luke 2:52). The Lexham Ministry Guides offer practical wisdom for the church.

My prayer is that you grow in humble appreciation of the rare honor and responsibility that Christ Jesus bestowed on you in the power and presence of his Spirit: "As the Father has sent me, even so I am sending you" (John 20:21).

Father in heaven, as in every generation you send forth laborers to do your work and equip them by your word, so we pray that in this our time you will continue to send forth your Spirit by that word. Equip your servants with everything good that they may do your will, working in them that which is well pleasing in your sight. Through Jesus Christ our Lord. Amen.

Harold L. Senkbeil, General Editor
September 14, 2020
Holy Cross Day

Prayer for Shepherding Those in the Valley of the Shadow of Death

Since the earliest days of the church, Christians have used holy Scripture to shape and inform their life of prayer. The structured prayer below invites pastors and laity to pray for those walking through the valley of the shadow of death. It can be used by either individuals or groups—in which case a designated leader begins and others speak the words in bold font.

In the name of the Father, Son, and Holy Spirit.
Amen.

O Lord, open my lips,
**And my mouth will declare
your praise.** Ps 51:15

Even the darkness is not dark to you;
The night is bright as the day,
for darkness is as light with you. *Ps 139:12*
The Sun of righteousness shall rise
  with healing in his wings. *Mal 4:2*

That God would grant his sheep faithful
  shepherds who will guide them through the
  valley of the shadow of death
That he would, through his shepherds, grant his
  sheep courage, healing, and times of feasting
  and joy in the midst of grief;
That he would hold his people even in the midst
  of death, be present to them in Word and
  sacrament, and so bring them to live with
  him forever;
Lord, in your mercy,
Hear our prayer.

That God would protect his people from anxiety
  and despair in the face of death;
That he hold before them death's defeat by the
  cross of Jesus as their only hope;
That he would grant shepherds and sheep both
  perseverance in times of deepest trial; that
  they may come together to the gates of the

Celestial City, there to live in happiness with the King.

Lord, in your mercy
Hear our prayer.

Our Father, who art in heaven,
Hallowed be thy name.
Thy kingdom come,
Thy will be done on earth as it is in heaven.
Give us this day our daily bread, and
Forgive us our trespasses as we forgive those
    who trespass against us,
And lead us not into temptation,
But deliver us from evil,
For thine is the kingdom, and the power, and
    the glory for ever and ever.
Amen.   *Matt 6:9–13*

Almighty God and Father, our lives are like the flowers which flourish in the field; when the wind blows over them, they are gone, and that place remembers them no more. In life, so teach us to number our days that we might gain a heart of wisdom; in death, hold us fast in your love that we might not be forgotten; and at the last bring us to share fully in the joy of resurrection. These things we ask in the name of him who died and rose again, that he might be the Lord of the dead and living, Jesus Christ, who lives and reigns with you and the Holy Spirit, one God now and forever.

Amen.

The Lord Almighty direct our days and our deeds in his peace.

Amen.

CHAPTER 1

Two Worlds

*A good funeral gets the dead where they need to go
and the living where they need to be.*
—*Thomas Lynch*

THERE WAS A TIME WITHIN LIVING MEMORY for some of us when a little book like this simply wasn't needed. I can just barely remember it. Growing up in small-town Canada in the late twentieth century, I recognized two centers of community life: the hockey arena and my local church. The latter welcomed newcomers when they were born (and when they were born again), helped launch them into adulthood, recognized their willingness to raise the next generation in marriage, and commended them to God when they died. This was what my church did. This was what all churches did.

In this world, a primer like this one on eschatology and the Christian funeral would have stood out as odd because *everybody* already knew what had to be done without having to be told. Everyone in my small town was connected to a church; the local community churches at a sociological level performed the same tasks despite differences in theology; the local culture supported and encouraged such connections and responsibilities. However, early on, I intuited this world was being supplanted. I can well remember my uncle giving an earnest testimony at a Sunday morning service, expressing worry for the future of our town when the local Agricultural Society decided to keep the Fall Fair open over Sunday. I couldn't articulate it at the time, but I now see that my uncle's concern pointed to a fracture between the local church and the local culture. A harmonious relationship could no longer be taken for granted. People would still be born, launch into adulthood and independence, marry, and die, but the relationship in which local churches were expected to perform the rites that assigned meaning to these events could no longer be assumed and would no longer be the same. From here on, culture and church would, from time to time, compete—and culture invariably would win.

This story is hardly new. It is the story of Western culture, narrated and re-narrated as the transition from a recognizably Christian culture (Christendom, for short) to modernity, postmodernity, and secularity. Two books tell this story powerfully. Charles Taylor's *A Secular Age* narrates a transition from two selves. The first, a "porous self," is one whose boundaries are permeable by both nature and supernature, a self who is open to the transcendent (or God) and believes in the possibility of miracles. The second, a "buffered self," is one who is open only to the material world, who may well continue to nod to God but no longer looks for divine intervention, and who counts miracle stories as fairy tales. In the former, the church is a necessary cultural actor, helping to shore up society's frame and function. In the latter, church is at best an alternative form of charity that other agencies manage more effectively, but more likely church is an eccentric hobby for older people. John Milbank's *Theology and Social Theory* argues more stridently that this new world is constructed not simply as a transition away from "Christendom" but the erection of "anti-Christendom," a culture grounded on a deliberate rejection of the Christian, largely Catholic, consensus that gave birth to it in the first place. While Milbank's and Taylor's accounts overlap, they do not agree at all points. Nevertheless, their general point is clear: while small-town Canada may be slow in catching up, the West is living in a new world where the old cultural consensus about religious values and Christian faith is gone.

In this new world, babies are born, adolescents assume adult responsibilities, young people partner and have children, and the old die. But there is no longer a shared sense of meaning assigned to these events by a common institution. The rites of passage are no longer uniform. Baptisms, confirmations, marriages, and funerals continue to happen—though at a frequency that discourages all but the most courageous clergy—but they have competition. And I'm not speaking of the competition that comes from having a mosque down the street and a Hindu temple two blocks over. Rather, it's what arises once sufficient numbers of people believe that these meaning-assigning tasks, the rites of passage, are malleable products formed by consumer desire and available for purchase.

In the old world, people were assigned identity by any number of factors—gender, race, faith, place, family trade, etc. Through the rites of passage, people became part of a story that began long before them and would continue after; they received what they were given and, hopefully, lived long enough to pass that along to the next generation. Changes happened undoubtedly, but at a much slower, if not to say glacial, pace. I'm not about to justify the abuses inherent in this arrangement, by the way. We are better off not defining people so rigidly as we once did. We are better off having, for instance, consigned race-based slavery to the dustbin. In the new world, identity is constructed. We can choose not only our trade and place with an ease unheard of a century ago—think about the hassle of Thanksgiving travel to get back "home"—but also our faith. We can pick bits and pieces here and there to assemble our own religion: cafeteria spirituality is well known and thriving. We can even, according to some anyway, choose our gender and our race. One might be forgiven for concluding that it sometimes seems that the only evil left is anything that might inhibit self-actualization. The new world is the world of the self-as-autonomous-consumer, the self that is no self until it makes itself through conspicuous consumption. This vision is not without its own anxiety-producing and abusive consequences.

Perhaps weddings are the most obvious place to look at just how far-reaching the intertwining of "rite-as-consumer-product" and "self-as-consumer" has become, but any clergy or funeral director will be able to signal how it is exerting an impact on their work too. I can remember when funeral homes in my home county self-segregated by denomination: Protestants took their dead to one funeral home, Catholics to another. There were no other options. Our small town remains—in ways both delightful and frustrating—achingly slow to catch up to modernity. But like most funeral homes over the last half century, ours has moved from Protestant to nondenominational to multifaith. We are not yet to the stage where the chapel is renamed a "celebration center," clergy are replaced by religiously uncommitted "celebrants," and the language of the funeral is completely eclipsed by the language of "celebrations of life," and for that I am thankful. But that day has come for many, especially in urban centers, and over time it will come here too.

This turn—astonishing in its rapidity—represents a fracturing of a close working relationship that was, in the old world, taken completely for granted: that of the clergy and the funeral director. Funeral homes have had to make changes because of the transformation wrought by the ubiquity of consumerism. As a result, clergy can no longer presume to have any special relationship with their local director. Every decision is now dictated by those making the arrangements. There may be a church funeral; there may be a chapel service; there may be a celebration of life at a local pub; there may be nothing at all. It is the funeral director's task to coordinate the particulars in each instance so that whatever happens is to the customer's satisfaction. Religion is now simply one among many options.

And it is this turn of events that makes a book like this necessary. It doesn't take a crystal ball or even keen observation to conclude that changes in culture impinge on how churches administer rites of passage to people. Specifically, clergy and other Christian leaders can no longer count on the culture to teach our people how to die. We cannot rely on a special relationship with our local funeral director as we prepare a family for death or arrange a funeral. This is no fault of theirs; clergy and churches are merely one consumer option in the designer-funeral, among many. And that means, when we walk with a spouse, a child, or a family through the valley of the shadow of death, we are going to need to recover and teach them an old language and reinvigorate a set of practices to help them make sense of what they are going through.

WHAT I'VE JUST DESCRIBED BECAME AN EXISTENTIAL reality for me in the middle of a funeral liturgy at an Anglican parish in Sudbury, Ontario, Canada. I was both newly ordained and new to the parish. My Archdeacon, Anne, had connected me to the local funeral director, Gerry, and he, in turn, took me under his wing—a kindness for which I will always be grateful. "You're wet behind the ears," he said at our first breakfast meeting, "so I'm going to throw lots of funerals your way. The Archdeacon says you need the practice." True to his word, he did.

In my first year of ministry in Sudbury, I had a funeral weekly. In the 2010s Sudbury was still a city living on the memory of its Christian past. Immigration had brought people of other faiths to be sure. But most residents were either churched or dechurched, with nary a "none" in sight, which meant that a Christian funeral was still a high-demand product. So I met with bereaved relatives, planned funerals (which ranged from the elaborate in church liturgy to the simple chapel remembrance service), and offered what little counsel I could to families in the most difficult of circumstances. I received the practice I needed.

One morning, my office phone rang. "Tim, we have a funeral for you. The family's name is Johnson. Ask Gwen who they are." Click. Conversations with my funerary mentor were always brief. My administrative assistant, Gwen, on the other hand, was always good with people's backgrounds. She had been a member of the parish for fifty years when I met her and an employee of the parish for twenty of them. At the time, it seemed to me that she had seen every parish family through generations of baptisms, weddings, and, yes, funerals. So when I told her the family name, she immediately knew who I was talking about. "They're an old parish family. The kids and grandkids haven't come to church for twenty-five years, but the lady you'll bury was a regular before that." I gathered more background information, the address and phone number, called the family, set up the appointment, and went to see them.

At their home, the family greeted me kindly. They told stories about their mother and grandmother and faithfully relayed the readings and hymns she had chosen. I went through the Anglican liturgy, explaining the order of service and what the family could expect. We talked about whether and where they would participate and so on. They gave the impression that while they cared deeply for their matriarch, honoring her Christian faith was simply part of honoring her. Faith was not a meaningful part of their own lives. As the appointment wound down, I prayed with them, they thanked me, and I left. I patted myself on the back on my way to the car. I was getting good at this.

Then came the service. The liturgy unfolded: Scripture sentences and procession, hymn, welcome. I was about halfway through the homily when I looked deliberately at each immediate family member, expecting to see expressions of grief or wistfulness. Instead, I saw complete bafflement. The dechurching of this family had been devastatingly effective; they had no idea what was going on. Not even half-remembered Bible verses from Sunday School long ago had registered. "I have nothing to say to these people," I thought in the middle of my homily. Our hour-long meeting had not given them the hooks they needed to hang the liturgy on, to help them make sense of what was happening.

What was happening? At its best, the Anglican funeral liturgy gives the language of centuries of Christian faith—the language of the church—to a family in mourning. It's a tool, if you like, to help families bring a shattering limit-experience within a community of shared speech, symbols, and meanings. The language of the church enables them to commit their loved one to God, who is infinitely just and merciful; to mourn and to move; to mark the loss even as they transition their loved one from the community of the living to that of the dead.

On this day, however, it dawned on me that I might as well have been speaking Chaucer's English. They were catching the odd word, but for them, it was an unknown tongue.

THIS LITTLE BOOK IS A DIRECT RESULT OF THAT experience. The first part is theological and theoretical. Some practitioners will be tempted to skip this first part and jump to the practical information in the second. I urge you (if that is indeed you) to resist. For the loss of the language of personal eschatology is not only a problem for the laity and unchurched or dechurched people who come to you for help. It's your problem too. (When was the last time you heard or preached a sermon on death?)

Part I offers a series of four reflections on the classical last things—death (chapter 2), judgment (chapter 3), hell (chapter 4), and heaven (chapter 5)—from a pastoral-practical theological level. Part II will move to more concrete matters: family preparation (chapter 6), the liturgy (chapter 7), the homily (chapter 8), and aftercare (chapter 9). The aim in each of these chapters is to bring the theological work of Part I into the realm of practical application, and so to integrate good theology and good pastoral practice.

"You shall know the truth, and the truth shall make you odd," wrote Flannery O'Connor. Christians in the West are at the start of a journey into oddness that will persist for quite some time. I am convinced Pope Emeritus Benedict XVI is right to say that this is part of a purifying process through which the church will emerge chastened, holy, and smaller. But there's no doubt it's going to be painful. Whether this is so or not, whether the valley into which we are now walking is long or short, we need to recover our in-house language to explain ourselves to ourselves and show others why we do what we do. And that includes dying, death, and the funeral.

I hope when readers finish the book, they will conclude that the Christian way of dying may make us seem odd. That's true and becoming truer daily. I hope readers will come to share my conviction that late modern Western Christians can die and mark death in a specifically Christian way.

Part I

Pastoral Theology

CHAPTER 2

Death

I was a pauper born, then to primate here raised,
now I am cut down and served up for worms.
—Henry Chichele (epitaph),
Archbishop of Canterbury

FOR ALMOST FOUR CENTURIES, PROTESTANT and Catholic theology were content to leave eschatology—that is, the study of the last things or the end times—to, well, the end. The reason is straightforward enough. At its extremes, the Reformation kindled an apocalyptic imagination that not only instilled hope for the coming of the Lord, but also led to immoral and sometimes violent actions both in expectation of that coming and in a desire to hasten it. Will the new Jerusalem come to Münster?[1] Playing with eschatology was, in the days of the Reformation, to play with fire: it may well have generated light and heat, but when not carefully tended, it burnt down the house.

This apocalyptic zeal was but an echo of the millennial fervor that gripped Europe five centuries earlier, when, much like our own Y2K, the turn of a millennium fired eschatological expectation and culminated in serious social disruption. The churches of the Reformation, both Magisterial and Catholic, regarded these apocalyptic moments with a jaundiced eye and could violently crush them when deemed necessary. Eschatology retreated to the final chapters of academic textbooks.

It was only in the second half of the twentieth century that eschatology emerged from its millenarian exile. World Wars I and II were the death knell of a culturally accommodated Christendom that could no longer distinguish itself from European society. And into that context, the existential theology of Rudolf Bultmann and early Karl Barth proclaimed the immanent and imminent coming of the Lord, the existential inbreaking of the kingdom of God into the present. The Lord is come again in the Word, and we need to adjust our lives accordingly.

THE RETURN OF ESCHATOLOGY AND
THE APOCALYPTIC IMAGINATION

Eschatology was back. Barth and Bultmann's students, notably Jürgen Moltmann and Wolfhart Pannenberg, left their mentors' existentialism behind but kept eschatology at the core of the Christian dogmatic project. Longing for the coming of the Lord would be expressed in rehearsing the mighty acts of God in and through history—the transformation of the present world, the goal. Their students, in turn, have given us the various theologies of liberation, which seem to supplant longing to see the coming of the Lord and his kingdom with striving to bring in the kingdom and its justice altogether. By the late twentieth century, the traditional loci of death, judgment, hell, and heaven were replaced by hope, the future, and liberation, all in dialogue with Marxism.

As these theological movements worked themselves out in seminaries, churches, and ecclesial communities across Europe and in the Protestant mainline of North America, fundamentalist and evangelical churches took a different turn. In their eschatological imagination, the second half of the twentieth century was the era of *The Late, Great Planet Earth*. What had been a fringe doctrine since the 1830s among the Plymouth Brethren became, thanks to Hal Lindsey, Dallas Seminary, the Scofield Study Bible, and the music of the early Jesus Movement, a central transdenominational preoccupation—dare I say distraction—for millions of believers. The four traditional eschatological topics were replaced by esoteric theories about a secret rapture, the great tribulation, the millennial kingdom, and the last judgment. Lengthy discussions based on detailed, perhaps picayune, exegesis of Daniel, Ezekiel, and Revelation ensued. America's, Israel's, and Russia's involvement in these soon-to-be-unfolding events, the identity of the antichrist, and the general timing of the (true) church's rescue were plotted on increasingly detailed Bible study charts. The first foray into the broadly popular imagination was signaled by the *Thief in the Night* movies that traveled the church circuit in the 1970s and reached their zenith two decades later with the best-selling *Left Behind* novels and then movies.

As we move into the early twenty-first century, the eschatological impetus is morphing again. In some corners, the old eschatological fire still burns—ideologized on the left by progressivism, and on the right by Make-America-Great-Again

Trumpism. On the whole, however, the eschatological tide seems to be receding. The Protestant
mainline in both Europe and America is discover-
ing just how hard hope can be in the face of demo-
graphic cratering. Pragmatic strategies for survival
are replacing eschatology. Fundamentalist and
evangelical pop dispensationalism also seems to
be retreating.

In neither case, however, is this a return to
eschatological modesty. In the former, it rather
looks to me like exhaustion from trying to keep
the machine working with fewer people and less
wealth; in the latter, embarrassment at excess
and, frankly, comfort with the American Dream
silencing the longing for the coming of Jesus. N. T.
Wright, a rare author who transcends the theological divide, is almost single-handedly trying
to reinvigorate the eschatological imagination in
both popular (*Surprised by Hope*) and academic
(*History and Eschatology*) publications; but it is as
yet unclear to me whether, despite his impressive
sales, he is succeeding at the congregational level.

On the other hand, in the post-Christian West,
eschatology is now in the open. One need not be
a climate change skeptic to any degree to observe
the near-millenarian fervor that accompanies

climate-crisis predictions of a not-quite-imminent end of the world, the human race, or at least of the conveniences of late modern capitalism. There is something deeply human about doomsday prophecies and the notion that catastrophe can only be averted by taking the right action. Right. Now. And so we find ourselves at an odd cultural moment: while the emerging post- or anti-Christian culture of the late modern West lives in increasingly eschatological and apocalyptic imagery, *the* eschatological community, charged with proclaiming Christ until he comes, is too exhausted or embarrassed to carry out its evangelical task.

Do you suffer from eschatological exhaustion? Embarrassment? You may well have good reasons. But even in this odd moment in which we live, Christian pastors are not free to set eschatology aside. We are not because we continue both to walk with people to their deaths and to accompany their families afterward. Helping people prepare to die and to mourn their loved ones isn't simply a matter of technique. It is *the* lived space where eschatology ought to inform pastoral practice. Death, judgment, hell, and heaven are not the last loci of the theology text to be skipped over for the sake of other more pressing matters.

Pastors have a responsibility to help their people recover the imagination and the language of Christian eschatology for two reasons. First, if the Christian gospel does not convert their imagination, it will be converted by the wider culture. Second, if that happens, evangelization fails. We need to teach our people eschatology as part and parcel of their and our discipleship and their and our mission. We need to stoke in their hearts a longing for and an expectation of the coming of Christ—who has come again in the resurrection, who comes again and again in Word and sacrament, and who will come at last to make evident to every creature what is already true: he reigns.

MEMENTO MORI

"Remember that you will die." It was a phrase a slave was said to have whispered into the ear of a victorious Roman general as he returned home in a triumphal procession with his plunder and people, bringing glory to his city. These five words certainly are a good remedy for keeping the ego in check if nothing else. More than that, they are an invitation to consider both the inevitability and ubiquity of death and to live in the light of that reality. They are an invitation to enter fully into life. Stoic philosopher Marcus Aurelius, perhaps the greatest emperor of pagan Rome, phrased it aptly: "Do not act as if you had ten thousand years to throw away. Death stands at your elbow. Be good for something while you live and it is in your power."[2] On this much at least, Christian faith and Stoic philosophy agree. Death is inevitable and ought to impinge upon how we live this life.

This chapter begins our exploration of personal eschatology by turning to the least speculative of the last things: death, and specifically, it's existential impact, the way North Americans (don't) talk about it, and the rich vocabulary the Christian tradition provides to help us order our lives in its light. The central claim I'll unpack in the sections to follow is simple: preachers and pastors have a duty to their congregations to teach them about death and to hold before them with regularity that they will die.

THE INTRUSION OF DEATH

In his thick book on sin, Lutheran theologian Ted Peters introduces his readers to the concept of anxiety and argues that this vague disease is produced by the awareness that our existence is, in the great scheme of things, insignificant.[3] Not only will we die, but when we do, the world will carry on as if we never existed in the first place. Such feelings can be triggered by the most trivial of events: being cut off in a grocery line or (pastors take note) having a visitor sit in "your pew" at church. Many times, however, the triggers are far more momentous.

In my own life, the existential reality of my eventual end intruded quite forcefully three times. The first was the birth of my oldest son, Calvin. It was Rachel's first pregnancy, and all went well, except for one thing: our boy was too comfortable in her womb. At twelve days past due, we went for an ultrasound. After the test, the tech announced, "He's just fine in there and still growing," to which my wife replied, "He's coming out now." Her doctor agreed and induced labor. It was long, difficult, and in the end required assistance. When Calvin was born, the umbilical cord was wrapped around his neck, and he was not breathing. Instead of the joyous moment we envisioned, when the doctor would place our newborn son on his mother's chest, he was whisked away by the attending physician and a nurse who cleared his lungs. Soon Calvin was crying (or at least trying to), and all was well. But for a moment, it looked like we were in real trouble. It was probably only thirty seconds long, but in the forever in which hope and grief were suspended, death came into the room. I was immediately aware of just how fragile life is, how little control I had, and how "we face death all day long" (Ps 44:22 NIV). We may concoct elaborate strategies to deny it or distract ourselves from it, but there are moments when the strategies fail, and death lets us know he's there. Waiting.

The second time was the death of my father. Diagnosed with terminal cancer in 2016 and told to put his affairs in order, my dad turned a three-month prognosis into thirty as he and my mom fought the disease with a determination that was both fierce and joyous. I learned that when it comes to dying, you need to embrace a rather hard realism if you're going to have any happiness at all: with defeat inevitable, you learn to surrender ground as slowly as possible and take joy in each delay that comes. My father's death was not sudden. Although he would never, ever have prayed the Litany of the Saints, one of its old petitions, "From a sudden death, deliver us, O Lord," was granted to him—such that when he died, all that had to be said beforehand to his wife, sons, grandchildren, and friends had been said. His affairs truly were in order in a way far deeper than his doctor could have imagined. When my dad died, he began the long wait for the resurrection in true eschatological hope. We laid his body to rest in confidence, knowing that my dad's heart already rejoiced in his future resurrection (Ps 16:9–10). When my father breathed his last, I was acutely aware of the enmity of death—and its defeat.

The last was my fiftieth birthday party. My wife had gone to a great deal of trouble to give me an event to remember. My friends were there— some came from quite a distance to feast on pizza and chicken wings and enjoy a private concert by one of my favorite singer-songwriters, Randy Stonehill. When he started into "Keep Me Runnin,'" a song about being chased by a relentless God,[4] my thoughts turned to the evasions of grace we all embrace—like parties that both mark and mask the fact that there are more days behind me than ahead. My son almost died; my dad did; and I will. No matter how well I cover up my tracks, whenever I look back, I see death gaining on me. Although I don't want to, I am going to die.

THE NORTH AMERICAN WAY OF DEATH

Allison Krauss and Union Station, one of my favorite American roots music bands, recorded an old bluegrass standard that begins, "Everybody wants to go to heaven, but nobody wants to die."[5] Never underestimate the power of bluegrass music to shine a humorous light on a harsh truth. This opening line is close to the heart of what once was the reigning civil religion of North America. The truth of its first statement is obvious to anyone working with the recently bereaved. Grieving people have little difficulty talking about a wonderful afterlife, even if they don't actually believe in it.

In my work at a local funeral home, I had such conversations all the time. They ranged from the sentimental to the profound with people whose piety fell anywhere on the continuum from devout to nonexistent and formal to utterly idiosyncratic. Everyone—even confessed atheists, in my experience—wants their loved ones to go to heaven. While they may be more modest about their own eternal destiny—describing heaven in terms of a hope, however slim—most of the people I talk to are quite confident that heaven is where their recently deceased dear ones have taken up residence. Everybody indeed wants to go to heaven. I'll have more to say about that in chapter 5. For now, let's consider the second part of the song's line.

"Nobody wants to die": this one is a bit more complicated. Contemporary North Americans have a dysfunctional relationship with death: we avoid it until we no longer can, and then we embrace it with a passion that would have alarmed our predecessors. Except in specific circumstances, many North Americans don't have the vocabulary to even talk about death, much less have a serious conversation about it. This is true even in churches, where one might hope the topic would come up from time to time. When was the last time you heard or preached a sermon on the inevitability and ubiquity of death? Conversations with parishioners who are not dying where death is the topic for spiritual direction or prayer are rare. I am ashamed to say that in my ministerial experience such sermons and focused conversations are almost nonexistent. I did not start talking about death with congregations regularly until I took up work in a funeral home. I may be wrong, but I expect my experience is pretty typical.

However typical such reticence may be today, as a society we were not always awkwardly silent on the subject of death. My grandmother spoke often and easily about death, not least because she was so used to it. Her mother died when she was eight; she lost one child in infancy and another at six years; she lived through the influenza epidemic of 1918 and both world wars. And her experience was hardly unique. In the nineteenth and early twentieth centuries, every family in my community was at one time or another touched by a tragic, early death: young women in childbirth, young men in farming accidents, children from illness in infancy. Their stories are etched in simple monuments at the local cemeteries I am privileged to visit in my work. (I am particularly struck by the sheer number of monuments dedicated to children.) People talked about death more often, even half a century ago, because it was more present than it is today. And death may well become easier to talk about as our culture becomes attuned to the "deaths of despair" among the North American working classes that today are driving life-expectancy rates down for the first time in over a century. But we're not there yet. And while I do wish we North Americans, and especially Christians, were better at talking about death, this is not how anyone wants to see the vocabulary recovered. How have we arrived at this strange place?

A significant reason stems from the North American way of death—from the idiosyncratic way we initially avoid and then embrace it. We can group three avoidance strategies under the label "trivialization." The first is to deny it—we do not die. Recall the euphemisms in which we couch death. Loved ones pass on. They go home. One of the most popular poems for memorial cards in my local funeral home puts the issue plainly: "Do not stand at my grave and weep. ... I am not there. I did not die."[6] The transition is from one form of life to another, one invariably better than this one, one that looks a great deal like an extended family reunion. Whether such a reunion is a legitimate hope for the afterlife—or the life after life after death[7]—is a question we'll take up later. For now, it is enough to say it is animating and comforting for grieving families to believe death is a trivial interruption in an otherwise happy life.

Perhaps the most obvious way we express our denial is the collapse of the word "funeral." We no longer mark a death by ritually moving the dead from the community of the living to the broader community of the deceased. Instead, we hold a celebration of life that looks a great deal like a retirement party where the guest of honor is conspicuously absent. Lately, Christian "celebrations"—again speaking only from my own experience—seem to lack a christological focus. Heaven is described as a reunion with a spouse, parents, extended family, and friends. There may well be good reasons for conceiving heaven as involving a reunion of sorts; this idea can be found in many ancient and modern Christian prayers. However, problems arise when such talk displaces far more important themes of union with Christ even in death and the hope of sharing in the Lord's resurrection through death into Life in its fullest. For the Christian, death is not a hiccup between two modes of living that are largely continuous. Participation in collective cultural denial does us no good, whether in speaking to ourselves amid grief or to others amid theirs.

A second way North Americans trivialize death is at once more subtle than outright denial and more acknowledging of its reality: distraction. Our culture takes a level of unprecedented leisure available to nearly all income levels, and we frenetically fill it with flash and fury, ultimately to keep us from thinking about life's inevitable end. Death is reduced to a plot device in our favorite novels, TV shows, and movies. Over against this are increasingly countercultural Christian claims about the need for rest, solitude, and contemplation. I once read of a Trappist monastery that expanded the distance of church and culture on this point to the maximum: when a brother dies, his grave is not prepared; the next one is. His body fills the grave prepared at the previous brother's death. There is a continually open grave in the monastery graveyard, an always-available reminder that death's creep has not ceased; it will come for another in the community soon. The question such a disjuncture invites is: Which community is better able to embrace this life and face the mystery of death fully and hopefully? We'll take that up later.

The third way we trivialize death is to medicalize it—to treat it as a medical problem that will one day be fixed. In the past, such hopes were embodied in fringe movements like cryogenics, in which wealthy, terminally-ill people were invited to have their remains frozen at the moment of death in the hopes of reanimation at a future time when whatever killed them was curable. Today, such movements are more mainstream. In January 2019, during a talk at Wycliffe College, an Anglican seminary at the University of Toronto, Dr. Geordie

Rose challenged his largely Christian audience to let go of any hope of personal immortality traditionally conceived. Instead, this pioneer in the fields of quantum computing and artificial intelligence proposed thinking of the soul as a pattern in the brain, eventually capable of transference to an artificial matrix. Death would die on the day souls could be built and uploaded into a computer.

However close the transhumanist hope of transcending death might or might not be, the temptation to treat death as the failure of medical intervention is especially strong in North America. Death no longer happens in the home; it happens in the hospital. It is no longer an inevitable end; it is the failure of medical professionals to extend life. "Don't let the bastard win!" shouts Hawkeye Pierce to a patient hovering on the threshold of life in one of my favorite episodes of *M*A*S*H*.[8] More humorously, I once saw a billboard advertising a sketchy health product with the tagline, "Helping to reduce the mortality rate." Advances in medical care notwithstanding, the rate is steady at 100 percent. The bastard always wins.

Eventually, awareness of our mortality catches up to most of us. And on that day, the strategies of trivialization fail. The diagnosis, the tragic "before-her-time" death, the close brush through accident or illness, stops us short. We can no longer deny, distract, or medicalize. In the past, that day presented an opening for faithful Christian witness by Christian clergy or others to the hope afforded by union with Christ in his death. Anxiety would become the occasion for presenting the gospel of grace. Indeed, it continues to happen in large parts of North America where the vestiges of Christian culture persist.

In our urban centers, however, and stretching tentacle-like into "flyover country," is a new movement to objectify death. No longer a mystery over against which human life derives meaning, whether in Stoic or Christian fashion, death is an inevitability that need not take us by surprise. When we can no longer deny it, we believe we can control it and even, thereby, come to worship it.

In Canada, the horror euphemistically dubbed Medical Assistance in Dying (MAID) became legal in 2016. Canadians were assured that it would be limited to adults with a short life expectancy experiencing unbearable suffering. However, talks are now underway to extend those boundaries to include "mature adolescents" and those whose suffering makes the prospect of a long life unbearable, including the mentally ill. Thus far, the claims of various advocates for mental health and disabled persons—that such extensions would lead to the cultural acceptance of the old notion of "life unworthy of life"—have fallen on deaf ears.

One case in British Columbia has exposed the provincial government's willingness to extend insurance coverage to those requesting MAID but not to those asking for palliative care.[9] In this whole debate, the bureaucratic assumption is that death is now one more government service and, accordingly, scorn is heaped on those who might think it's not. In some strange way, to engage in the argument over euthanasia's permissibility is to admit that the debate is already lost. The only hope is to organize a dignified retreat and carve out whatever social space bureaucratic creep leaves those who disagree, who believe that the elimination of suffering cannot be equated with the elimination of the sufferer.

Having thus turned death into an object that the government wields over its citizens, it is but a short step to worship it. Death is now the great deliverer from suffering, and MAID doctors are the high priests who usher the faithful into its fearful presence. We can see the degree to which the cultural imagination has embraced this awful notion in the sitcom *The Good Place*. Positing an afterlife without God (the Judge is a burrito-eating reality TV addict who, while hilariously played by Maya Rudolph, has no resemblance to God as traditionally understood), its main characters eventually escape from the Bad Place only to find boredom in the Good Place. What to do? In the comedy's final season, the solution is presented: if any want to stay in the Good Place, they are free to do so, enjoying whatever pleasures it affords them as long as they wish. But once their afterlives are eclipsed by ennui, there is a way out: a doorway to Nothing. Suicide. Death delivers all who seek him from the unbearable irrelevance of eternal life. Nobody wants to go to heaven; everybody wants to die. And until then, we dance on the edge of the abyss.

This is our new moment, what John Paul II called "the culture of death."[10] Richard John Neuhaus famously insisted that politics was downstream of culture.[11] If that's true (I admit to being convinced), then the political battles now being fought (and lost) signal that the culture has already radically changed. What some sociologists call "expressive individualism" doesn't get to the core—the cult—of the culture. Christians are witnessing the birth of a new anticulture, one predicated on the deity of death, one with its own priests and ministers. It is on this canvas that a Christian understanding of death needs to be rearticulated.

The Christian Way of Death

A Christian understanding of death is not nearly so instrumental and certainly not as deifying as the one just described. Neither does it trivialize or objectify it. In the Christian imagination, death presents us with the mystery of life held in the hands of God—life that is not our own, that is fragile and limited. It presents death as the great severer of all loving relationships, as the punishment for sin, and as the final enemy. That's the bad news. And it's where we must begin.

In our current context, we must begin here lest we trivialize death and so lose our capacity to speak meaningfully about it. So let's start with a simple observation: death is not an inconvenient hiccup in one long, perhaps eternally extended, happy life, but rather the end. The oldest strata of the Old Testament affirm this. Whatever comes after (and we'll discuss what comes after) ought not to be seen as undoing this basic recognition.

In the stories of the patriarchs, the goal and good of this life were bounded entirely in this life. The ideal was to see the covenant faithfulness passed on to the next generation and the next—to work and prosper, to bounce grandchildren on one's knee, and then to die old and full of years and be gathered to the ancestors. *Sheol* in Hebrew (or *Hades* in Greek) was a place of witless shades and mindless mutterers, home to good and evil alike, cut off from the presence of the God of Life, and from where no one gave him praise.

In this much, the early Israelite understanding of death resembled very much that of Homer and the great Greek myths. Little, if anything, could be said about "after death"; whatever it was, it wasn't good. It wasn't oblivion, but it wasn't life either. Happiness was entirely a bodily reality. In the New Testament, this view was represented by the Sadducees, the temple elite, who insisted that in their narrow canon (the five books of Moses) there was no promise of an immortal soul or a bodily resurrection. The good life to be attained in faithfulness to God was attained in this life.

This simple but by no means naïve view of death and the goodness of this life is developed by later strata of the Old Testament and Jesus' teachings, to say nothing of his death and resurrection. But wherever we end up, we must start here. Death is the end. And that means that heaven as an uninterrupted family reunion simply will not do. Death is a break with life.

It is, then, the severer of loving relationships. A familiar biblical metaphor deserves full and serious reflection here. To die is to be cut off from the living, to be cut off even from God:

> I am overwhelmed with troubles
>> and my life draws near to death.
> I am counted among those who go down
>> to the pit;
>> I am like one without strength.
> I am set apart with the dead,
>> like the slain who lie in the grave,
> whom you remember no more,
>> who are cut off from your care.
>
> (Ps 88:3–5 NIV)

To "go down to the pit" is in some way to be at once utterly alone and with the dead. And that means our goodbyes to our loved ones are final. And frankly, it's bad for us to minimize that.

The Bible recognizes death—the end of life and the severer of relationships—as the consequence and wages of sin. This is a fate we have brought upon ourselves by our rejection of the God of Life for idols. In other words, death is a punishment that is not so much wielded by God as permitted by God. God's wrath, in its purest expression, is to allow us to experience the consequences of our own abuse of his gift of freedom and the rejection of his gift of life. We surrender our life step by step to our sin, and we die. All that remains is the sin that consumes us from the inside out.

C. S. Lewis offers a powerful portrayal in his parable of the afterlife, *The Great Divorce*. On his guided tour of heaven, Lewis overhears a fellow ghost complaining about all the hardships she had to endure in life, and he can't imagine that she ought to be condemned to hell simply for that. She needs only to be treated kindly to be redeemed. George MacDonald, his afterlife tour guide, responds:

> The whole difficulty of understanding Hell is that the thing to be understood is so nearly Nothing. But ye'll have had experiences. … It begins with a grumbling mood, and yourself still distinct from it: perhaps criticising it. And yourself, in a dark hour,

may will that mood, embrace it. Ye can repent and come out of it again. But there may come a day when you can do that no longer. Then there will be no you left to criticise the mood, nor even to enjoy it, but just the grumble itself going on forever like a machine.[12]

One way to understand hell—which we'll explore later—is to conceive of it as the death of the self even as the self's sin continues into eternity. The Bible speaks of death as the end, as severer, punishment, and enemy—the last enemy, in fact (1 Cor 15:26). And the last bit of bad news is that this last enemy will defeat us. Always. "Did we in our own strength confide, our striving would be losing."[13] Luther's hymn puts the matter starkly and accurately. When finally confronted by the ravening maw of death, before whom even the universe must succumb, perhaps all there is to do is to dance on the edge until we tip over into blessed oblivion. No Promethean raging against going quietly into the good night will arrest the inevitable. We will all acquiesce. While we might take a different route to get there, we Christians must acknowledge that the deification of death is not far wrong. Indeed, it is half right. Did we in our own strength confide, the striving would be losing. The most for which to hope is a final hand that makes our slip into Nothing as painless as possible.

But the Bible does not stop with the bad news about death. It rereads all of the above in the light of the life of Jesus. In doing so, the Bible at once recognizes the reality of the bad news and daringly asserts that it is, in God's ultimate goal, good news—such that death is no longer simply the end but is also a new beginning. This is not because of anything inherent in human beings. Christians do not believe—as the great neo-Platonic philosopher-mystic Plotinus did—that sloughing off our bodies frees our immortal souls to return to our true disembodied home. Rather, for the Christian, death is, in all its awful final weightiness, the completion of our identification with the Lord Jesus in this life. Death is an identification stamped on us in our baptisms: "Do you not know that all of us who have been baptized into Christ Jesus were baptized into his death?" (Rom 6:3). Our identification with Jesus, marked by our baptisms, means that for Christians, death is indeed the end of this life—not as an abandonment into Nothing but the final abandonment into the One who tasted death for all, and so removed its sting. It is the fullest abandonment into Christ, and as such, is an abandonment into Life more abundant than we can now ask or imagine. Saint Paul continues, "We were buried therefore with him by baptism into death, in order that, just as Christ was raised from the dead by the glory of the Father, we too might walk in newness of life" (Rom 6:4). This abandonment of life for Life through identification with Christ begins even now, and carries on, in some way, forever. Thus, Dietrich Bonhoeffer's last recorded words are spoken for us all: "This is the end. For me, the beginning of Life."[14]

We can press this further. As our abandonment—not to Nothing, but to the good care of the Lord Jesus—death is not the great severer of relationships but the transformation of all relationships through union with the risen Lord. As we have seen, the bad news of death precludes any imagining of heaven as an extended family reunion. It sets in its place union with Christ and says, this is our true end, the goal toward which we, in grace, were created to strive toward and finally attain. My wife powerfully experienced this truth several years ago when contemplating heaven while reading *The Great Divorce.* At one point, she had conceived of heaven as a place where she would be reunited with her mother, who died a year before we came to meet; later on, as a mother herself, she viewed heaven as a place where she would continue to know and love her children. But Lewis provoked a discomfiting question: "Why is union with Jesus not enough in itself?" The good news of death is that it marks the completion of our union with Christ begun at our baptisms. If we are reunited with our loved ones, drawn up together with even the saints and angels of every age, it is only insofar as we share in a common union. It is the union with Christ, who is our Life, that transforms the severer of relationships into a greater, more powerful union.

As the fullest moment of our union with Christ foreshadowed in our baptisms, death for the Christian is finally the embrace of eternal Life. Death is not an abandonment to Nothing, whether fearfully, defiantly, or happily, but an abandonment to the Lord, who calls the things that are not as though they are, who by his Spirit, fills us with his Life. So yes, death is the final enemy, and against him, in our own strength, the battle is indeed lost.

Were not the right Man on our side,
The Man of God's own choosing.
You ask who that may be? Christ Jesus, it
    is He;
Lord Sabaoth His Name, From age to age
    the same,
And He must win the battle.[15]

Luther's mighty hymn gives us the tools with which to read death in a Christian way. It is Christ who defeats death, and in so doing, transforms it into a new beginning, a union (and hopefully reunion) in the fullness of the divine love. In Christ alone, death becomes a gateway to eternal Life. And that is good news indeed.

Conclusion

None of this, of course, means that for the Christian the prospect of dying is undertaken without fear, without anxiety, without difficulty. Dying, even for the believer, is hard work. If our Lord himself can say with a troubled soul when confronted by the prospect of his own encounter with death, "What shall I say? 'Father, save me from this hour'?" (John 12:27). No, the prayer of our Lord in Gethsemane is the prayer for all who die in the peace of Christ: "My Father, if it is possible, may this cup be taken from me. Yet not as I will, but as you will" (Matt 26:39 NIV).

In my experience with dying people, I have seen people whose lives and confessions left me in no doubt about their heavenly home seize upon Christ and rest in their union with him, and I have seen others, sometimes even more saintly, express fear. My father, who was a godly example to me and many, asked my wife whether he was really going to heaven shortly before he was moved into palliative care. I am reminded of the disparate experiences of Hopeful and Christian, the main characters in John Bunyan's allegory, *Pilgrim's Progress.* When they came at last to the Celestial City, there was one final barrier: a river whose current was strong and whose bed was deep. Exhorted to trust in the King of the City and cross the river, they began to wade. Christian called out to his friend, "I sink in deep waters, the billows go over my head; all his waves go over me." Hopeful replied, "Be of good cheer, my brother; I feel the bottom, and it is good."[16] Dying is hard work. And the invitation to rest in Christ, or in Bunyan's fine phrase, to trust in the King of the City, is for some like Hopeful, easy. For many of us, though, Christian's difficult transition resonates more.

Whether we in our final moments emulate Hopeful or Christian, the goal of the Christian death is the same: the surrender of life to Christ, to the one who is Life, who will not let his chosen ones languish in the grave but will bring them into resurrection. Only from the deep truth of our present union with the Christ who comes for us at death can we move on to contemplate what happens after: judgment, hell, and heaven. And we turn there next.

CHAPTER 3

Judgment

*A true opium of the people is a belief in nothingness
after death—the huge solace of thinking that for our
betrayals, greed, cowardice, murders we are not
going to be judged.*
—Czeslaw Milosz

THE PREVIOUS CHAPTER BEGAN TO SKETCH A
personal, existential eschatology with a simple
observation: we are all going to die. Barring the
advent of the last day, death is the end for all of
us. We observed how recognizing our mortality
can produce anxiety; looked at cultural strategies
for avoidance, delay, and denial; and recalled the
Christian invitation to face our inevitable deaths
squarely. Of course, that's easily written. Facing
inevitable mortality, especially when it's imminent,

produces a range of responses. Having sat with dying people and with their families for over a decade, I've seen reactions swing from rage to fear to resignation to acceptance to hope. Even if basic Christian teaching on death is clear, believers' reactions are not, nor should they be. If our Lord could express fear in the face of death, if he could ask to be delivered from his final battle as he did in Gethsemane, should we expect anything else from our brothers and sisters? From ourselves? It is simply not the case that Christians so internalize the good news that death is defeated that we greet joyfully the moment of our complete identification with Christ that leads us into the greater presence of God.

Nor is it the case that nonbelievers die badly. I have known two atheists so committed to their convictions that they greeted death—at least in my presence—with a truly enviable peace. Few of us, Christian or not, greet the news of our impending death with the equanimity of the Scottish Enlightenment philosopher, David Hume. When James Boswell visited the famous agnostic on Sunday, July 7, 1776, to pay his final respects, Hume was dying of cancer, his hours now numbered. Expecting to find a man on the threshold of eternity soberly wondering what awaited him, Boswell found Hume awake, lucid, engaged in conversation, and in good humor. When he gingerly probed Hume's thoughts about the afterlife, Hume's conviction was made plain: he was no more bothered by his nonexistence in the future than by his nonexistence before he was born. Boswell, himself a believer, left Hume's deathbed deeply unsettled, and though he tried twice more to speak with him, this was their last conversation. Why was Hume the unbeliever accepting of his end while Boswell was shaken?

The answer lies in differing assessments of the common question: What happens after we die? Hume's conviction was a comfort to him: oblivion awaited; that is all. Hume's conviction, however, remains a minority, albeit a growing one. In his sermon "The Weight of Glory," C. S. Lewis speaks eloquently of the universal longing to be known and recognized beyond death. We want to be remembered. Lewis takes this as evidence that something of us persists.[17]

At some point, every parent encounters the question, "What happens next?" Perhaps it is raised in a fairly simple situation: the death of a beloved pet. Sometimes, though, it can be much more complicated: the death of a grandparent, parent, or even a friend. Whenever they ask, the little people want assurance that what they are watching unfold is not, in fact, the end of the object of their affection—that it is a mere interruption, that there will be a reunion of sorts in some kind of afterlife. But will there be? In the last chapter, we observed several strategies that our culture has built up precisely to avoid this very question. But it still intrudes upon us at key points in our lives. It is always lurking, waiting again for an opportunity to press itself upon our consciousness.

Pastors and Christian leaders ought to welcome the question when it comes, whether in the mature reflections of an adult or in the straightforward posture that only a child can muster. After all, if the Christian tradition invites us to look at death fully in the face and see there an enemy whose eventual defeat is not only sure but is, in fact, already accomplished, then we must go on to speak about what follows to whomever will listen. And that is just what the remaining chapters of Part I attempt to do. This chapter will focus on judgment: the traditional Christian claim that at death, an individual judgment for the deeds done in the body takes place, and that this judgment fixes our eternal destiny—either as an endless descent away from God, from grace, and toward Nothing, or as a no-longer-encumbered ascent into grace, God and ever-thicker Reality. Christian eschatological shorthand calls these alternatives hell and heaven, respectively.

THE IMMORTALITY OF THE SOUL

It is precisely at this point that many Christians find their words beginning to fail. Speaking about death may be uncomfortable, but it is not metaphysically difficult. Of the four great last things, it is the least speculative: there is a body from which life has departed that grounds our thinking—wherever our thoughts might end up—in this world. Dealing with death is, at a basic human level, profoundly pragmatic; it's moving past the practicalities of death that is more problematic. In the past, the Christian tradition spoke easily of an immortal soul that survived personal death. Many of the revivalist gospel songs I grew up on took it for granted: "Some glad morning, when this life is o'er, I'll fly away."[18] Personal immortality displaced "the resurrection of the body and the life everlasting" as the believer's hope as expressed in the Apostles' Creed; it was one of those cultural givens in the waning days of Christendom, so speaking about it was easy. One did not need to be especially devout to affirm that God would assess the deeds of this life at the threshold of the next and assign a place accordingly.

Today, when the metaphysical body/soul dualism that seems to undergird this way of thinking and speaking is itself under strong attack, it is increasingly difficult to give words like "soul" any coherent meaning. Increasingly, the default cultural position is a hard materialism. For growing numbers of people, the soul is, as we observed in the previous chapter, at most a pattern of brain activity that ceases when neurons stop firing. If there is any immortality to be hoped for, it is the transhumanist vision of neural patterns uploaded into artificial-intelligence matrices upon bodily death—an eternal "life" in a virtual reality. While the mind/brain distinction continues to provoke interesting discussion in philosophy and neuroscience, in broader life, those philosophers and scientists who identify mind and brain have the better press agents. Those of us who affirm (whether philosophically, empirically, or both) a mind/brain dualism—the existence of an immortal soul, an "I" that persists after my body and my brain have died—have been on the back foot for some time. We must begin with the question: Is this a bad thing?

We cannot preempt the conclusion that the cultural turn against the immortality of the soul is automatically a bad thing. It may well be that traditional Christianity's affirmation of the soul's immortality is itself a belief better discarded. Several theologians—notably, N. T. Wright, a New Testament scholar and former bishop in the Church of England—argue that the soul's immortality, as traditionally understood, distracts us from authentic biblical hope for the resurrection of the body. If this is true, maybe this cultural moment presents believers with an opportunity to scrape some unhelpful barnacles off the ship of faith. The metaphor is deliberate and can be expanded. The nub of the criticism is that, as the Christian faith navigates history, barnacles attach themselves to its original biblical authenticity. In the providence of God, however, cultural moments expose these barnacles, allowing us to remove them. Old barnacles come away; while new ones may well be discovered at the next dry dock, the church's journey can continue.

What we encounter in the doctrine of the soul's immortality, so the argument goes, is the intrusion of Platonic forms of thinking into biblical thought, leaving us with a gospel that Wright sums up in a perverse paraphrase of John 3:16: "God so hated the world that he killed Jesus."[19] The material world, and especially the human body, is evil or base. From it, humans need to be delivered. Salvation is such deliverance from materiality. For human beings, this means leaving our bodies behind at death for a disembodied eternity with God in heaven. Now there are two caveats that must immediately be made: (1) I have heard some Christian sermons and songs that express themes very much like those I've just mentioned. (2) The tradition itself—even as expressed in Augustine's doubtlessly neo-platonic thought—rejects views that pit the soul against the body. The reasons are straightforward: they deny the reality of creation's goodness and the love of God disclosed in Jesus and especially on his cross, and turn the gospel into, frankly, its opposite. I am, thus, sympathetic to the critique. The question is: Is the cure—leaving behind discussions of the immortality of the soul (and the closely related intermediate state between death and resurrection) as unbiblical accretions—actually worse than the disease? The answer is yes.

AFFIRMING IMMORTALITY

First, for all of history up to the second half of
the twentieth century, people experienced life as
"nasty, brutish, and short."[20] Any walk through an
old graveyard bears this out. Why would they not
want to leave this life behind for the promise of a
better one? If the hope of a disembodied heaven
displaced that of a bodily resurrection over the
centuries in the piety of many, it was not without reason. Of course, this is often pointed out by
the critics: the dismal prospects of this life worked
against a material conception of what came next
and toward leaving this life behind. To be trapped
in matter has meant, for the vast majority of human
beings, to be trapped in bodies subject to disease,
decay, and death. The old bluegrass hope is truly
transcultural: "When the shadows of this life have
gone, I'll fly away. Like a bird from these prison
walls I'll fly. I'll fly away."[21]

However, the challenge to the critics is that
the same criticism once uttered is easily enough
reversed: it is only as science and the global growth
of wealth lengthened lifespans and raised more
people out of poverty that bodily resurrection has
made a comeback. Might it not be that, in a few
decades, the same criticism will be turned against

the anti-immortalists? Namely, that their conception of a bodily material resurrection looks a lot like a longing for this world only slightly improved, because they don't want to leave this largely comfortable life behind. Having attained the American Dream, we wish to see it perpetuated into eternity. Of course, this first response is not a defeater to the criticism in any way. It is merely offered as a request for breathing room. Having not walked in forebears' cruel shoes, let's not judge them too harshly.

Besides, they might not have been as far from the Bible or biblical hope as is often presented. I'll come back to that further on. Before I do, I need to offer a second, more technical response. The criticism—too much Plato, not enough Bible— seems to assume that ancient cultures were discrete entities that did not overlap then and ought not to overlap now. It further holds that we can easily distinguish (in this case, at least) between Plato and the Bible, reject the former, and affirm the latter. But is this the case? Was there *ever* a purely biblical faith, a purely biblical culture standing undefiled over against the Greeks? You'd be hard-pressed in the pages of the Bible to find that the answer is yes. The Scriptures themselves come into being making use of the forms of thought at hand, at points adopting them, at others modifying, at others undermining. But the notion that biblical faith—whether that of Abraham or St. Paul or ours—emerges in a cultural vacuum, is corrupted by history, and can be purified at providential points is difficult to sustain under the evidence. The church is an ongoing event in history, always adapting, adopting, converting, and rejecting wherever it finds itself. Before leaving this notion, we can sharpen it further. I have yet to read a compelling response to Pope Benedict XVI's conviction that St. Paul's providentially directed turn west (Acts 16:6–10) made the encounter with Greek thought inevitable. Just because an idea can be traced back to Plato—or, more broadly, Greek modes of thinking—does not mean that it is therefore false or antibiblical. Indeed, it may have been encountered at the direction of providence.

And in the case of the immortality of the soul, one is hard-pressed to demonstrate this dichotomy, which brings me back specifically to the Bible and its cultural environs. It looks as though the notion of an immortal soul emerges both in Greek literature and in the Old Testament around the same time, for the related reasons but also independently of each other. The afterlife of the Homeric epics strongly resembled that of the earliest strata of the Hebrew Bible. It was Sheol. Hades. The grave. It was the realm of witless spirits to where even the most heroic were banished and from where none would return. To be sure, the Greeks and the Hebrews responded to the inevitability of the grave very differently. For Homer, the good life was one that garnered enough glory and renown to perpetuate the memory of one's name in this world, a far cry from the biblical apex—seeing the covenant faithfulness of God passed on to one's children and grandchildren and dying old and full of years. But that's not the point; the overlap in the conceptions of afterlife is.

What Homer and the early strata of the Bible could not address was the problem of justice. Homer tried by straightforwardly asserting the capricious nature of the Olympian gods. With gods and the fates being what they are, there is no such thing as final justice. Life, however heroically lived, is ultimately tragic. Paris and Achilles both are heroes, demonstrated in their feats of valor. Though they fought on opposing sides, they will both be remembered long after their deaths. For the biblical writers, the dilemma was sharper:

given God's covenant faithfulness, one ought to expect the righteous to prosper and the wicked to fail in this life. But such is not the case. Why do the righteous suffer and the wicked take their ease? Fully one-third of the Psalms pose this question in some form or other, as do the Prophets. Plato's notion of immortality evolves as an attempt to ground the possibility of the city—a life together in community—in a conception of justice that trumped the fickle will of Zeus with a vision of the Good. For the biblical writers—we might think of Job, the Psalms, the servant songs of Isaiah—that final justice lay in God's covenant faithfulness that itself transcended death.

The immortality of the soul emerges in the Bible and the Platonic tradition for the sake of justice, whether conceived as the covenant faithfulness of God or as the ground of a fully functional city or community. Once these similar notions come into contact in the deuterocanonical period (texts that Protestants too quickly and too blithely ignore, even if we do not accept them as canon[22]), some sort of cross-fertilization is bound to take place—and that is, of course, what happened. All this to say, we cannot discretely distinguish between Hellenism and Holy Writ, as some critics appear to believe. Indeed, as the early liberal Adolf von Harnack realized and put into action, once we start editing out the Greek, we will move behind the Nicene and ante-Nicene fathers to the pages of Scripture themselves.[23] To return to the naval metaphor above, if we are not careful, along with the barnacle that needs removal, we may well take some of the poor ship's hull while attempting to recover biblical purity. The supposedly tidy distinction between Bible and Plato isn't so tidy at all.

JUDGMENT, JUSTICE, AND ME

So let's set aside that issue to probe a far more interesting one. What does the immortality of the soul have to do with judgment? For both the Old Testament and some Hellenistic philosophies with which it intertwined during the intertestamental period, underlying the concern for justice is the assumption of personal continuity after death. For the Platonists, the pursuit of the Good persists past death but begins now. In this world, the pursuit is evidenced not only in the near-ascetic life of the philosopher-king but also in the possibility of a life together: a city where each in his station is oriented toward this transcendent goal. The fickle gods were not, finally, ultimate. If they existed at all, they would finally be accountable to the Good in some way or other. So it was that Socrates could drink the hemlock, confident that his vision of justice would be upheld over against the Athenian city fathers, their gods, and their ridiculous charge of atheism. Socrates faced his death evenly because of his confidence that that he would be shown to have been in the right all along.

He would be vindicated. In other words, justice would be upheld, but it would be so with respect to Socrates, and ultimately with respect to *me*. Here we can return to the biblical idiom. The wicked may well lie on beds of ease while the righteous suffer outside the city gates. This injustice may well be left unaddressed in this life. Still, the Lord will not turn his face away forever; even after death, he will turn his face toward me and vindicate me. Not only will vindication take place, but it will be done in public—in front of my enemies who themselves will be put to shame. From a hope for divine justice derives personal continuity beyond death and public vindication of both the righteous and the God who lives in covenant with them. From there it is but a short step to the hope of a bodily resurrection that we find expressed, for example, in Daniel 12:2, which says, "Multitudes who sleep in the dust of the earth will awake: some to everlasting life, others to shame and everlasting contempt" (NIV). In other words, we don't get to resurrection in the Bible apart from some sort of immortality, and what grounds both is the covenant faithfulness of God toward his people, both collectively and individually. Far from an unbiblical alternative to biblical resurrection, immortality is resurrection's prerequisite. To borrow from the philosopher Ludwig Wittgenstein, we are not free to kick away the ladder after we have climbed it.[24]

The Old Testament's vision of immortality can thus be plotted along a chronological line. It begins with a simple vision of the grave and of the covenant faithfulness of God to his people in this life. The good life was realized in this world—a long life with many descendants living in the land of promise. In the face of the empirical failure of this simple view, a view of God's covenant faithfulness, and of the individual and the nation as the objects of such faithfulness, emerged that held that death was not the end. The true end was the vindication of God—both as God's vindication of his people against their enemies and God's vindication of his own justice against its deniers—an end unencumbered by time or even by death. If God keeps his covenant promise, something of the individual and the people persisted beyond those barriers to share in its keeping. In its final form, that eschatological hope was expressed as a bodily resurrection so that God's covenant faithfulness could be demonstrated in public.

There is, then, an eschatological development that affirms personal immortality in some form or other, culminating in a bodily resurrection unto judgment. And if that's the case, the New Testament is wrongly read as the displacement or supersession of the (pagan, Greek) immortality of the soul by the (authentically biblical) resurrection of the body. They are not alternatives between which we must choose. The longing for justice, for vindication, and the presupposition of personal continuity is indeed in the Bible. Likely at points in dialogue with Hellenist thought, and certainly on its own terms in others, this longing requires us to speak of the soul's immortality. What then does the witness of the New Testament add? Just this: Jesus.

JUDGMENT, THE JUDGE,
AND FINAL JUSTICE

The New Testament is rich in the imagery of judgment. (One may think, for example, of the inbreaking of God's kingdom in the Synoptic Gospels, the judgment of the Son in the Johannine literature, the hope of the resurrection at the parousia in the letters to the Corinthians and Thessalonians, the justification of God in Romans and Galatians, the cosmic Christ of Ephesians and Colossians, and, of course, of the final judgment at the climax of Revelation.) Clearly, a thorough examination of the New Testament witness isn't possible here. While what follows hopefully does justice to the whole of the canon, I am going to limit myself to two passages of Scripture, both from the Gospel of Luke: the parable of the rich man and Lazarus (Luke 16:19–31) and the penitent thief (Luke 23:32–45).

Turning to the rich man and Lazarus, some preliminary observations must be made. And the first is often brought up by those critical of what I am about to do: mine the parable for its eschatological insight. It is a parable, not an eschatology, and that must be kept in mind—even as the parable of the sower (Luke 8:4–15) is a parable and not a lesson in agrology. Second, it is a parable ultimately about Jesus—note references to the resurrection—and the hardness of his hearers' hearts, not about the nature of the afterlife. These observations require us to keep our aims relatively low. Still, we must say that whatever its value *as a description* of the afterlife, this is a parable about judgment. Without an afterlife—not simply as a device but in reality—the parable makes no sense. Let's now unpack this parable further.

First of all, it is striking that Jesus takes up an intertestamental understanding of the afterlife without commentary. Abraham's bosom as a place of reward for the righteous dead, separated by a chasm from hell as a place of suffering for their oppressors, is not invented by Jesus; it is simply part and parcel of the eschatological milieu in which he conducted his ministry.[25] Now, as to whether the metaphysics is ultimately correct, we need not worry. We need only say here that Jesus takes this for granted as much as he takes farming for granted in the parable of the sower. If this vision is ultimately false, pernicious, demeaning of God and humanity, one might be permitted to wonder why our Lord deploys it without a qualm. It simply is there. And that means, it seems to me, that Jesus *at the very least* uses this imagery of reward and punishment to affirm the reality and gravity of a postmortem judgment. In some sense, our fates are determined at death based on how we have lived in this life.

Second, this postmortem judgment may well overturn what appears to be the natural justice observed in the material world. That is to say, the final judgment may well call into question our own ways of judgment. At the outset of the parable, it appears that the sore-covered beggar, Lazarus, is sitting under the wrath of God. If the blessing of God is a prosperous, long life passed on to many children and grandchildren, Lazarus clearly has done wrong. One can almost imagine the disciples' question regarding the blind man redirected to him: "Rabbi, who sinned, this man or his parents?" (John 9:2). At the same time, the rich man, dressed in purple and fine linen, living in luxury, is just as obviously enjoying the present blessings of the covenant God made with his people. And yet, a strange reversal takes place at death. Expectations are utterly overturned when it is Lazarus who is taken to the place of peace while the rich man descends to torment. Thus, this parable not only affirms a final judgment, but in so doing, indicts all previous ones as at best partial, and at worst unjust. On what basis does this turning of the tables take place?

This question brings us to a third observation. At a surface reading, the parable itself suggests that the judgment will be based on relative lack versus relative wealth. Recall the words of Abraham to the rich man: "Son, remember that in your lifetime you received your good things, while Lazarus received bad things, but now he is comforted here and you are in agony" (Luke 16:25 NIV). But a closer reading suggests a verdict more complicated than this. The rich man pleads for his brothers, hoping that if Lazarus risen from the grave preaches to them, they will repent. But, says Abraham, they have the Scriptures. If they do not repent based on these, they never will, even if someone were to rise from the dead. The criterion of judgment, then, is not wealth but repentance. It is not the sharing of wealth with Lazarus that would have redeemed the rich man, but the repentance which was the redistribution's source; sharing is the visible evidence of authentic repentance. And, warns Jesus, some hearts will be so hardened that the call to repentance will be ignored even if delivered by one risen from the dead.

And here, fourth, the parable delivers its blow by bringing judgment from some point in the future ("the time came … " [Luke 16:23]) to the hearers' immediate present: like the rich man, some of the hearers of this parable will not repent and believe when the opportunity is given to them. They have not only the witness of Moses and the prophets. They have one in front of them who will die and rise at their hands, calling them to the same change of life. Yet in their refusal to recognize and obey him, they pronounce their fate to be that of the rich man even now: they will go to hell. In other words, repentance is inextricably tied to hearing and obeying Moses and the prophets as they are given to us by the one risen from the dead—namely, Jesus. Repentance is defined in terms of belief in Jesus. He is both judge and the criterion of judgment.

When we move to the story of the penitent thief, similar themes emerge. Recounted only in Luke 23, this story opens with clearly defined marks of judgment. Consider the following. The men crucified along with Jesus are anonymous; they are known only as *kakourgoi*, literally, workers of evil (Luke 23:32). Sentence on them is passed—they are crucified along with Jesus (v. 33). Jesus himself pronounces judgment, albeit one running against the stream of the scene (v. 34). The soldiers are oblivious to that judgment (v. 34); the mob passes their judgment (vv. 35–38). One thief echoes the judgment of the crowd: "Are you not the Christ? Save yourself and us" (v. 39). He hopes to find in Jesus an overturning of the judgment passed on him. The other, however, speaks quite differently. He recognizes the justice of his and his companion's fate and the injustice of Jesus' (vv. 40–41). The entire setting is one of judgment, both just and unjust, passed and borne.

In that pregnant moment, the thief passes his own judgment on Jesus. "Jesus, remember me when you come into your kingdom" (v. 42). Not only does the thief recognize that Jesus is innocent of the crime of blasphemy, but because he is innocent, the thief accepts Jesus' identity as Messiah— the one in and through whom the kingdom will come. The thief judges rightly: Jesus of Nazareth is indeed the King of the Jews, on the threshold of entering his kingdom. With him there can be no bargain, no if-then, no save yourself and us. There is only a plea to remember. *When you come in your power and glory, please don't forget me.*

At the climax of the scene, Luke shifts to focus on Jesus. Having opened with the judgment of the

Lord on the whole scene ("Father, forgive them" [v. 34]), he now passes judgment on the thief. The soldiers, having done their duty, uncaringly cast lots for the clothes of the condemned, utterly ignorant of the forgiveness begged on their behalf. And the mob, having judged that Jesus is condemned both by human and divine justice, mocks him without mercy. The penitent thief has alone judged rightly. Jesus' response begins with the emphatic *amen soi lego*: "Pay attention to what I say to you!" It is as though the judge has rapped his gavel and is about to pronounce sentence. "Today you will be with me in paradise" (v. 43).

Themes reminiscent of those found in the parable immediately emerge. First, in the unfolding horror, Jesus alone is the judge, indeed the only true administrator of justice amid injustice. His judgments of forgiveness on his killers and welcome to the penitent thief stand as testimony to the profoundly counterintuitive nature of God's justice when set against human standards. Thus, we have an indictment of all human judgment as at best partial (the thieves' sentence is in some sense just, and is not, in fact, set aside by the Lord), or at worst unjust—we have crucified the Lord of glory.

Second, there is an affirmation of a postmortem judgment. Jesus welcomes the thief into paradise, a well-known eschatological equivalent to Abraham's bosom—the place of reward and rest for the righteous dead. Third, note here a significant change. The thief is not welcomed, as Lazarus was, into Abraham's presence but into the presence of Jesus: "You will be with me" (Luke 23:43). Fourth, although there is no obvious repentance—how could there be, given the moment—like the parable's conclusion, the judge's verdict hinges on the recognition of Jesus as the Lord of the kingdom. Finally, the consequences of the judgment are immediate. The thief will see them unfold "today."

Even though we have looked at but two short passages from one Gospel, we have glimpsed the fullness of judgment in the entire canon. The New Testament does not supersede or overturn notions of judgment in the Old Testament but brings them to their fullness by placing Christ where he belongs: at the center. Jesus is the justice of God breaking into this world; in judgment, he overturns our false judgments by forgiving and welcoming sinners into his kingdom both today and hereafter. This is the power and wisdom of God that confounds the wise and routs the powerful. This is good news.

Union with the Judge

Before concluding this chapter, we must return to a theme unfolded above: death as the moment of complete identification with Christ. If this is the case, and, as we have seen, Christ *is* both the judge and the judgment of God, then death is the moment of our own judgment. Everything leading up to this moment—the small decisions in which we turn toward or away from grace, all the small interventions of the Holy Spirit in our lives—takes on final, ultimate significance. For it is at this moment that we encounter the flame of love who consumes all that is wood, hay, and stubble, leaving only gold, silver, and precious stones (1 Cor 3:12–15). So it is that the judgment, even if a painful encounter, is one of great hope for the believer. For it is then that our union with Christ will be perfected, and we will be drawn even more fully into union with him.

I am reminded of Eustace Clarence Scrubb in C. S. Lewis's *Voyage of the Dawn Treader*, who stole an enchanted bracelet that turned him into a dragon. Eventually resigned never to be a boy again, Eustace tries desperately to reform his character, but he only grows in his "dragoness," and the enchanted bracelet begins to cut into his foreleg, causing him great pain. One night, he is woken by a lion who, though he is much smaller than dragon-Eustace, terrifies him. The lion bids him, "Follow me." They walk together to a pool, and Eustace is invited to bathe. First, however, the lion bids him to undress. And Eustace tries to scrape off his dragon scales. They come off easily, only to expose another layer of scales underneath. Eustace is a dragon all the way down. "You will have to let me undress you," says the lion, and Eustace submits. As Eustace tells his cousins later, "That very first tear he made was so deep that I thought it had gone right into my heart. And when he began pulling the skin off, it hurt worse than anything I'd ever felt. The only thing that made me able to bear it was just the pleasure of feeling the stuff peel off."[26]

Eustace's encounter with Aslan, of course, is a description of our encounter with Christ. At the moment we realize we cannot change ourselves, we are changed by the just and saving judgment of the Judge. And such judgment is both incredibly painful and ultimately good. It restores us to ourselves. While this may rightly be read as the moment of conversion, it also points to the moment of ultimate encounter, when we identify with Christ in death and greet him as our judge.

Whatever pain may be involved, it is something for which believers ought to hope.

And this raises a concluding question.

WHY IS JUDGMENT FEARED?

In 2009, hot off the literary successes of the four horsemen of the atheist apocalypse (Richard Dawkins, Christopher Hitchens, Sam Harris, and Daniel Dennet), a British atheist organization known as Humanists UK ran what they called the Atheist Bus Campaign. Using it to promote their cause in London, they described it as one of their best campaigns ever. And in the decade since, it has been duplicated across the world, including in major North American centers. You don't have to be English or British to be familiar with its slogan: "There's probably no God. Now stop worrying and enjoy your life." God, it seems, is a cosmic killjoy who inspires fear to make people "be good." But what if "being bad" is fun? What if whatever pleasures we enjoy and God disapproves of can be indulged because there is no God? No doubt, these are the kinds of questions that the campaigners wanted to provoke.

But they rest on an odd supposition: the judgment of God is something to be feared. This is, of course, far from what we have described above. Where Charles Wesley could invite his congregations to sing, "Rejoice in glorious hope! Our Lord and judge shall come"[27]; there would be no such tune for these folks. To move away from judgment, they urged an embrace of oblivion. And my reaction to that was, and remains, one of profound sadness. Could it be that so many greeted the campaign slogan with relief because, deep down, they knew that, were God to judge, they would not be among those who rise at his judgment?

It is this troubling question that brings us to the threshold of our next chapters on ultimate destiny.

CHAPTER 4

Hell

The choice of every lost soul can be expressed in the
words, "Better to reign in hell than serve in heaven."
There is always something they insist on keeping,
even at the price of misery.
—C. S. Lewis

THIS IS THE CHAPTER THAT I DIDN'T WANT TO
write, the one that was the hardest to put together.
I hope the reason is immediately clear: hell, con-
trary to AC/DC's song, is a bad place to be. More
importantly, it is also a difficult matter to think
through—and not only for emotional reasons.

Whatever emotional neuralgia may be evoked
by serious contemplation of Jesus' words about
outer darkness, a fiery furnace, and weeping
and gnashing of teeth (as found, for example, in

Matthew 13), hell is an even greater challenge for theological thought. It implies an eternal blight on God's good—indeed, reconciled and restored—creation. It appears to imply that some who desperately want to go to heaven are nevertheless excluded. How can these things be? Hell makes no sense! Hell is cruel and unusual!

I'll come back to that question and those charges below. I want to begin by acknowledging a criticism that some might wish to make of this chapter at the outset, namely that of question-begging. This chapter assumes the tradition on hell is largely right and true—and that, for the critic at least, is precisely what needs to be overturned.

The debates over more inclusive or even universal doctrines of salvation have simmered slowly in Christian thought, at least since the third century. Nevertheless, the mainstream Christian tradition (both Eastern and Western), while it has accommodated various views of the afterlife for those who spurn God's grace, has agreed that universal salvation simply is not an option. From Origen to Gregory of Nyssa to Jacob Böhme (the now largely unknown father of modern universalism) to David Bentley Hart, today the defenders of universalism, no matter how eloquent, represent

at best an ongoing "minority report." I have neither the time in this short book nor, honestly, the
acumen to address the debates. I leave that to others
(most notably, Michael McClymond).[28] I am content at this chapter's outset to place myself in the
nearly two-millennia-long Christian mainstream.
Whether clergy or other practitioners like it or not,
an awareness of the doctrine of hell will impinge
upon our care for the dying and the grieving, and
explaining it away is not, in the end, a pastoral help.
So, yes, I am indeed begging this question. But I am
doing so self-consciously and relying on "a great
cloud of witnesses" (Heb 12:1) that begins not with
Augustine, but with our Lord himself.

In doing so, I am not, of course, endorsing those
lurid depictions of eternal punishment from the
medieval era. Hell, like heaven—as we'll see in the
next chapter—is as much an imaginary construct
as a Christian doctrine. And some imaginings
can be easily left behind without calling fidelity
to the scriptural witness or the credal tradition
into question. Think about this. Whenever hell
is mentioned today, many imaginations continue
to conjure versions of some of the "doom paintings" from medieval hospitals. These were depictions of the last judgment in which the enthroned

Christ welcomes his resurrected saints into heaven and casts the risen rest into a hell full of R-rated, demon-operated torture devices uniquely suited to their sins. Many doom paintings render hell as a perversion of heaven all the way to the bottom. In their original intent, these paintings were invitations to the dying faithful to remain on the straight and narrow by holding out hope for and a healthy fear of what might await them. They are medieval versions of today's pictures of cancerous lungs legally required to be posted on cigarette packages. They mean to scare people straight.

And in at least one contemporary instance, one of these paintings accomplished its evangelistic purpose: it was as he looked at Rogier van der Weyden's *The Last Judgment* that Peter Hitchens began his return to Christian faith. He easily imagined himself among the damned, writing:

> Because they were naked, they were not imprisoned in their own age by time-bound fashions. On the contrary, their hair and, in an odd way, the set of their faces were entirely in the style of my own time. They were me and the people I knew. ... I had a sudden, strong sense of religion being a

thing of the present day, not imprisoned under thick layers of time. A large catalog of misdeeds, ranging from the embarrassing to the appalling replayed themselves rapidly in my head. I had absolutely no doubt that I was among the damned, if there were any damned.[29]

Hitchens's profound experience allows us to see how the paintings were intended to function—and did. Nevertheless, for most of us moderns, such depictions of hell have, by too many horror movies, an unfair scoffing at anything medieval and a general antisupernaturalism turned to the opposite of the painters' intentions. Their cartoonish depictions of eternal destruction—to our sensibilities—make the very notion of hell all too easy to scorn or ignore. Devils with pitchforks are, after all, Halloween fun for most of us. We can't take those images seriously. But to dispense with the medieval torture chamber is neither to deny its importance in its original context, nor to deny the Christian doctrine.

Hell as an implication of human freedom and moral responsibility before God remains even after the medieval torture chamber is set aside. And when presented as such, it sometimes succeeds in cutting through so much secular bafflegab to catch us up short. An exchange between Minister Jim Hacker and his principal secretary, Sir Humphrey Appleby, the main antagonists in the classic comedy *Yes Minister*, capture hell's ongoing moral gravity for at least some of us. The idealistic, naïve, and dim (if charming) minister has discovered that his government may be selling arms to terrorists. He wants to get to the bottom of it regardless of the consequences. His secretary, a Machiavelli in pinstripes, advises against it. Never ask a question when you don't know the answer in advance, he says. Let sleeping dogs lie. When Minister Hacker, his patience growing thin, insists that there is a fundamental point of good and evil at stake, Sir Humphrey counters, "Minister, government isn't about good and evil; it's only about order, or chaos." He adds that he has no opinion on right or wrong; his job is to carry out government policy regardless: "As far as I'm concerned, minister, and all of my colleagues, there is no difference between means and ends." This leads Minister Hacker to conclude, with a gravitas disproportionate to his usually flimsy character, "If you believe that, you will go to hell."[30] I have never heard a sermon on hell that has affected me so deeply as have those nine words.

About the nature of hell and its torments, this chapter has nothing more to say, and its eternal reality is from here on assumed. Hell is the destiny of those who, like Peter Hitchens before his return to faith and the fictional Sir Humphrey Appleby (whom we have all met in some form or other), have seared themselves against the responsibilities of freedom and the invitation of grace.

THINKING THE UNTHINKABLE

With that in mind, let's return to the first charge—namely, that even when shorn of its medieval exaggerations, the notion of an eternal hell as a space cut off from God's redeeming love and reconciled creation makes no sense. The charge can be set out simply. If the traditional doctrine of hell is true, then the traditional understanding of God as Redeemer and Reconciler of *all* is not. This part of eschatology rests on a fundamental contradiction that, for God's sake, needs to be resolved. But how?

Of the two solutions to be taken, the first is the more straightforward: dispense with hell altogether, whether by arguing that *all* are saved by Christ (Christian universalism) or by presenting death itself as the gate to life eternal (unitarian universalism). I have sat through too many funeral homilies that have taken either route. The second solution modifies the doctrine in terms of duration (hell, though perhaps ages long, is ultimately temporary) and/or purpose (hell's pains are redemptive, not punitive). Of course, the varieties of the second solution—which include annihilationism—are not so easily preached, even if they attempt to take the biblical witness more seriously. Whatever solution is taken, the charge can be tidily summed in this way: "God is good. There is no hell."

I am attracted to these sorts of arguments as any Christian with a heart should be. No one who has been overwhelmed by the love of Christ can gloat over the thought of a crowded hell. Varieties of universalism do not err in their desire to offer hope to grieving people. At their best, they seek to defend God against what they perceive as a grave moral calumny. At their core, they are convinced that a traditional understanding of hell not only contradicts God's power, goodness, and love, but also—precisely because it does so—defies all theological reason. Hell, at least in some form of the traditional definition, is irrational, and therefore, cannot be true. If it is to withstand scrutiny, hell must be made rational, must be made to comport with what we believe about God. And so hell becomes temporary and redemptive (i.e., it becomes purgatory), or it is dismissed altogether.

If we are going to respond to this argument, we must begin by granting the main objection. Hell is irrational. It makes no sense. Traditionalists err when we attempt to fit hell into the grand scheme of things, not least because, while the Bible speaks of hell, it never explains it but merely asserts it and moves on from there. Jesus' words in Matthew 13, which adopt his culture's understanding of hell and continue to give us our basic eschatological language, never explain. They simply assert. The wicked will be cast into outer darkness where there will be weeping and gnashing of teeth. No explanation is forthcoming. Why not? An answer, I think, can be found not in hell, but in the larger problem of sin. Hell makes no sense because sin makes no sense. It is theologically irrational. And as theologically irrational, it ought not to be. It is impossible.

Think, for example, about the fall story in Genesis 3. Adam and his wife are created with a will oriented toward the Good and desires shaped by and for the Good. They live in a verdant garden of uninterrupted fellowship with God, each other, and the created order. And yet when tempted, they fall. It makes no sense. As God's good creatures, there is no inner disposition that might make the serpent's offer attractive in the least. That they saw, took, and ate in disobedience to the divine command ought not to have happened. And yet it did. Further, the fall was predicated upon a lie: "You will not surely die" (Gen 3:4). And lies, by their nature, frustrate reason and reason's quest for understanding. They prevent reason from uncovering the truth. The root of sin is deception, which shrouds both its origins and final explanation in a horrible chiaroscuro. Sin cannot be explained. Just so with hell. It does indeed make no sense, and no sense can be made of it. On this, the traditionalist and the universalist ought to agree. Where they part is over just what to do about it.

Both solutions invariably leave the scriptural narrative behind. Whether we look at the Platonic speculations of Origen or the more Christian thoughts of his disciple, Gregory of Nyssa, at the esoteric Jacob Böhme or the evangelical Robin A. Parry, we inevitably find a commitment to a smooth system superseding the rough-edged biblical narrative. The mind of the church, however, in both the East and the West, has concluded that to "fix" this dilemma has meant to leave the scriptural narrative behind: "It has found itself obliged to concede that such an expectation of universal reconciliation derived from the system rather than from the biblical witness."[31] We are left with G. K. Chesterton's apt observation that while the best and brightest may wish to explain sin (and hell with it) away, it remains before us "as plain as potatoes."[32]

Sin and hell, then, are not speculations to be overcome by reason. They are realities overcome only by Jesus Christ. Not by Hegel's speculative Good Friday, in which thesis and antithesis are overcome in a greater synthesis, but, as Ratzinger insists, by the evangelists' real Good Friday, on the real wood of the real cross.[33] Sin, and accordingly hell, as traditionally presented, are indeed irrational. They are impossible possibilities. But in their absence, the good news of the gospel—sin expiated and wrath propitiated; victory won all for us, in our stead; violence and injustice overcome by love; indeed, the incarnation and atonement altogether—itself becomes senseless.

HELL AND THE HARD CASES

Let's move to the second charge, namely, that hell as traditionally understood (again, admitting various understandings within that umbrella) ultimately, cruelly, excludes people from God's kingdom who want to be there. Think about the millions who have throughout history died without hearing the gospel and about those who have been conditioned against hearing it as good news by the sins of God's people. In other words, think about hell's hard cases. If the first charge questions the rationality of God's creation, this one goes to the heart of God's goodness. If there is a hell, then God is not good.

This problem is not new in Christian thought. From Justin Martyr in the second century onward, Christian thinkers have sought to give an account of those who, though they did not live to hear the gospel of the Word incarnate, nevertheless responded to and followed that Word as he was revealed to their reasons, their consciences, and through the created order in other ways. They may not have entered fully into God's rest in heaven but certainly were spared the worst torments of hell. The thirteenth-century philosopher and theologian Gregory of Rimini, indeed, stands out as exceptional for holding to a strict Augustinianism all the way down. Those who die without baptism, including infants, he averred, suffer the pains of the damned. No wonder he was nicknamed by his enemies as *infantium tortor*, the torturer of babies.

Nevertheless, there is something distinctively modern about its current expression. From the later fathers through the medieval scholastics and Reformers, the challenge of the hard cases was often merely theoretical, writing as they did from within a Christian culture. The pastoral matter at stake for them was not "what about the noble pagan?" (Jews and Muslims were apostates and heretics respectively, i.e., those who had rejected the gospel) but "what has happened to my child?" as Gregory of Rimini's perverse pigeonholing indicates.

It is only after the missionary explosion that accompanied the colonial expansion first in the Catholic Reformation and then the Protestant Great Awakenings that the hard cases reemerge into Christian consciousness. Charles Freer Andrews springs immediately to mind. A Church of England missionary sent to India by the Cambridge Mission to Delhi in the early twentieth century, Andrews was quickly impressed by the vibrant spirituality not so much of Hindu thought but of actual Hindus. A strong, early advocate for Christian-Hindu dialogue, Andrews counted Mahatma Gandhi and philosopher Rabindranath Tagore among his friends. He reportedly described Sree Narayana Guru in this way: "I have seen our Christ walking on the shore of Arabian sea in the attire of a Hindu *sanyasin* [holy man]." Dubbed by Gandhi himself as "Christ's faithful apostle," Andrews never deviated from his own serious Christian discipleship; he nevertheless could not deny what he saw as God's grace at work in the lives of people who were not Christian believers. In the century since he first went to the subcontinent, Andrews's experience has been duplicated across the world as immigration patterns and ease of travel have brought what was once exotic and remote literally to next door.

In my own circles, C. S. Lewis's character Emeth is regularly invoked at this stage. A Calormene soldier and sworn enemy of Narnia, Emeth (whose name is the Hebrew word for "truth") finds himself at the end of *The Last Battle* confronted by Aslan the lion (Lewis's Christ figure) and despairs. The lion—whom he calls not by name but by title, the Glorious One—will surely know that Emeth served his own god, Tash, all his days. As a result, he will surely die, though happily as one permitted to gaze upon such beauty beforehand. He is shocked when instead of a sentence of death he hears, "Son, thou art welcome." The mighty lion then disabuses the soldier's confusion. He is welcome into Aslan's kingdom not because Aslan and Tash are one but because they are opposites. No one who seeks and does good—even in Tash's name—will be turned away. Or as Aslan puts it, "Unless thy desire had been for me thou wouldst not have sought so long and so truly. For all find what they truly seek."[34]

The cross-cultural encounters of C. F. Andrews and the nobility and goodness of Emeth cannot be used to frame a theological response. But they do sharply illustrate the difficult questions. Does hell await those who heard the gracious call of God through reason, conscience, and creation? Who responded faithfully to whatever light they were given? Or is such revelation sufficient only to damn? Is eternal separation from its one true desire the fate of the heart who longed for God but did not hear the gospel? Of course, the questions are leading. And yet, no Christian with a heart can dismiss them. Emeth is a literary stand-in for Gandhi, for Tagore, for Sree Narayana Guru. He helps me ponder my kind and generous Sikh neighbor. Is *that* their future?

The only way through these questions is, I am convinced, to hone them further, but in a way you might not expect. Over against Emeth, allow me to place another example from popular literature: Sam Cayhall. When we meet him in John Grisham's *The Chamber*, he is a thoroughly unrepentant racist and convicted killer awaiting the inevitable on death row. His words and actions garner no sympathy, whether from readers or his fellow characters. Even his lawyer (and grandson) Adam Hall, having taken up the case in a hope to understand his past, seems unable to sympathize with Sam. At a pivotal point in the novel, Adam discovers an old photo of a lynching, and among the crowd is Sam, then only a child. Adam realizes that whatever monster Sam had become, given his environment, he could not really have been something other than that. Of course, this does not excuse his crime—a bombing that injured a Jewish civil rights lawyer and killed his two young sons. But it does explain the context in which such a crime could be conceived and carried out. The poisonous racism that fueled Sam's rage and culminated in his crimes was inhaled with his first breath. His trajectory was set for him. This realization makes Sam more sympathetic to Adam, maybe even redeemable.[35]

Is hell the future of those who are conditioned by the circumstances of life against hearing the goodness of the gospel through no fault of their own? What of those who have been set on their own course by generations of horrific attitudes and actions well ingrained before they took their first breaths? What of those who have been abused by those who were ordained to bear Christ's love to them and so cannot hear of God's love without pain?

Here's my point: when it comes to hell, *every* case is a hard case. As David Bentley Hart puts it, "There are always extenuating circumstances."[36] That, however, ought not to drive us—as it does Hart—to speculative universalism as much as it should to reverent awareness of God's character: there is only one Judge. Of Plato or Caligula. Of Emeth or Sam Cayhall. Of Gandhi or Mother Teresa. There is only one in whom justice and mercy embrace fully and rightly. Only one who can take on the enormity of the task and, in the words of Abraham, do right (Gen 18:25). He is the one who expressed his infinite justice and love on the cross. God's love disclosed in Christ is just, and it is merciful, and it is costly. And we must entrust the hard cases to him.

We can press this further. The hard cases ought to drive Christian believers to reverent contemplation not only of God, but also of the precarious nature of their position. Even though the Scriptures themselves provide ample material that invites speculation about the hard cases when the question is posed directly, Jesus offers a troubling answer:

> He went on his way through towns and villages, teaching and journeying toward Jerusalem. And someone said to him, "Lord, will who are saved be few?" And he said to them, "Strive to enter through the narrow door. For many, I tell you, will seek to enter and will not be able. When once the master of the house has risen and shut the door, and you begin to stand outside and to knock at the door, saying, 'Lord, open to us,' then in reply he will say to you, 'I do not know where you come from.' Then you will begin to say, 'We ate and drank in your

presence, and you taught in our streets.' But he will say, 'I tell you, I do not know where you come from. Depart from me, all you workers of evil!' In that place there will be weeping and gnashing of teeth, when you see Abraham and Isaac and Jacob and all the prophets in the kingdom of God but you yourselves cast out. And people will come from east and west, and from north and south, and recline at table in the kingdom of God. And behold, some are last who will be first, and some are first who will be last." (Luke 13:22–30)

There is nothing here about the hard cases. Indeed, Jesus seems to think that such speculation is a distraction. *You* strive to enter the narrow door, he says. The nobility of Emeth and the wickedness of Sam may well, in my own self-centeredness, become a means to avoid far more troubling questions: Am I striving to enter the narrow door? Have I discovered the hard-to-find narrow way? Throughout the Gospels, our Lord presents hell as a warning to the presumptuous people of God, and that's where our emphasis ought to fall.

LIFE AS A TRAJECTORY

In a time when (with notable exceptions like Peter Hitchens acknowledged) most of us have either softened or set aside the New Testament language that medieval artists seemed to revel in, how does one talk about hell? Let me attempt to flesh out this answer: hell is the end of a life formed by a pattern of decisions to refuse God's gracious overtures. I am making two claims here: (1) human lives are, in the end, trajectories either toward or away from God, and (2) we are the same people after death as before. Let's take each in turn.

Several years ago, my wife took a course in Ignatian spirituality at a local Catholic university. Taught by the chaplain, a Jesuit, it was a short introduction to the spiritual exercises of St. Ignatius of Loyola. My wife loved it; I loved that she loved it. Mine was an experience of vicarious enjoyment as she came home and shared with me her experiences of the course. As I learned with her, I was fascinated by the notions of consolation and desolation, the emphasis on spiritual warfare, and the practice of *lectio divina*—slowly reading and meditating on a small portion of Scripture (usually from the Gospels) by imagining oneself into one or more of the characters and trying to see it from the inside. However, I don't speak for my wife when I say that none of these practices moved from being fascinating to a basic part of my devotional habits.

Except one. The practice that I took away from the course and continue to observe is known as "the examen." While the Jesuits are supposed to practice the examen twice daily, I have come to keep it as part of my bedtime routine. Here's what I do: as I settle into bed, I try to still myself and become aware of God's presence. Some days are better than others, but mostly, this practice involves breathing and letting go of the day's tensions. Once calmed, I review my day with two questions in mind: Where in my day was I most conscious of God's presence? And where in my day was I least aware of God's presence? As I do so, I attend to my emotions. How did I feel at points through my day, especially when God seemed to be close or distant? How do I feel about those points now? I then reflect with gratitude on my whole day and commit it to God's good care. Finally, I ask for God's presence to guard me sleeping and guide me waking, so that tomorrow might be better than today, at least in terms of my attention to the gracious presence of the Lord.

I certainly don't present myself as a master of the Ignatian form of Christian spirituality. Even as I look at my one takeaway, the daily examen, I see how my practice is idiosyncratic. Regardless of how imperfectly performed, it did (and does) teach me two valuable lessons about how to think about my life and those I have cared for as I have endeavored to pastor them. The first is that our everyday lives are made up of very few momentous or significant decisions, yet God comes to us all the same. Though the big events come, more often than not our lives are a series of small steps, small decisions, small routines, and small interruptions. And it is in these small places where we find God—if and as we are trained to see. On the other hand, if we are attuned only to what we might call "Damascus Road" interventions, we will surely miss the small ways God in grace comes to us every day.

The second lesson has to do with habits and identity and follows directly from the first. By practicing the examen, I have learned (and continue to learn) to look for God in the small things; further, the more I look for God in the small things, the more I find him waiting there. Just so, as I respond to God in the small things, it becomes easier to respond to God in the small things. In short, the more I seek, the better seeker I become; the more I respond, the more responsive I become.

I have discovered that becoming attuned to God's presence is not the province of those supernaturally gifted masters whom the tradition calls mystics. The difference between a St. Ignatius or a St. Theresa and the average disciple is one of degree, not kind. And that means becoming attuned to God's presence in the events and decisions of daily life, no matter how large or small, is rather like becoming a good piano player or a good carpenter. While there may well be certain natural affinities that help, seeking and finding God is about acquiring skills and practicing them under the guidance of someone "further up and further in" than myself.[37] As my seeking and finding become habituated, the more I become a person who both seeks and finds. I become what I do.

This spiritual dynamic is true for every human being. We are each on a trajectory of becoming more attentive or deaf to the Holy Spirit's overtures in the little things. We are always and everywhere to discipline ourselves to see and press into grace or to ignore and turn away from it. And whatever trajectory we've set ourselves on, the further we're on it, the easier it is to maintain—but the harder it is to divert. No one who finds themselves in hell will, I believe, be surprised.

Saying No to God

The second claim implied by my definition of hell is also straightforward: God's gracious invitation can be, and is, refused. Hell is a consequence of God's free gift. Again, this needs some spelling out.

Several years ago, on the Sunday before our local high school graduation, Rachel and I gave our parish grads presents—little things that would be useful for setting up college living arrangements, like a laundry basket, some kitchen items, and a bag of peanut M&Ms. I can't imagine being excited for a laundry basket and some tea towels, but our future collegians were. And good for them. Even if the present in itself was merely useful instead of spectacular, they seemed glad to know someone was thinking about them. Everyone loves presents.

Now, imagine coming to the tree on a Christmas morning. You're bleary-eyed. Dying for that first cup of coffee to get you through a busy day of unwrapping, church, turkey dinner, and all the rest. And your child comes up to you and says, "Where's my Christmas sacrifice?" Or you say to your child, "Why don't you start handing around the Christmas sacrifices?" Or your spouse says to you, "Oh honey, thank you for the sacrifice. It's just what I wanted."

At best, that appears to be a category confusion, a mixing of the festive and the ritualistic in a way that just doesn't make sense. So perhaps the first thing to say is that an ancient reader, whether Jewish or Christian or pagan, would have had no trouble understanding the previous paragraph. Where we moderns are utterly confused, for a reader from the fifth century before Jesus up to the fourth century after (at least), the notion of sacrifices given at Christmastime would be utterly obvious. What have we lost? The notion of sacrifice. We have no idea what a sacrifice is anymore. If we use the word at all, we use it as a metaphor. So we might say, "She works hard all day so that her children can go to university. What a sacrifice." She is doing something unpleasant in exchange for something greater. "He sacrificed his job in order to help his aging parents." He is giving up something good for the sake of something more noble. In our modern world of metaphors, sacrifice means relinquishing some personal good for the sake of someone else's (greater) good.

When we use the word "sacrifice," we certainly don't think of an animal ritually slaughtered. We don't think of an altar smeared with blood or a ritual burning where the smoke rises to God. For an ancient reader, on the other hand, that is exactly what a sacrifice was. At its most basic, a sacrifice was a gift offered to God in exchange for something else. A pagan general may go to the temple of Ares, the god of war in ancient Greece, and offer a sacrifice in order to get the god on his side in an upcoming battle. A Hebrew woman may go to the temple after childbirth and offer a sacrifice in order to be cleansed from ritual impurity (Mary did that in Luke 2:22). So in a celebration in which gift exchange was the central motif, using the language of sacrifice would make perfect sense to an ancient.

In the ancient mind, there is a deep interconnection between the divine, the sacrifice, the gift, and ties of mutual obligation. But it's not entirely confined to that world long ago and far away. Perhaps recalling the opening scene of my favorite movie of all time might help. It is the day of Connie Corleone's wedding, but the father of the bride, Don Vito Corleone, is not with his guests. He is in his darkened study listening to a heartbroken father beg him for justice. The father—a local undertaker named Bonasera—wants some boys who savagely assaulted his daughter to die. The don rebukes him for seeking his help only after going to the police didn't work. Furthermore, Bonasera asks for murder, which is not justice because the girl still lives. Here is the next segment of the conversation:

Bonasera: Let them suffer then, as she suffers. How much shall I pay you?

Vito: Bonasera, Bonasera. What have I ever done to make you treat me so disrespectfully? If you'd come to me in friendship, then that scum that ruined your daughter would be suffering this very day. And if by chance an honest man like yourself should make enemies, then they would become my enemies. And then they would fear you.

Bonasera: Be my friend, Godfather. [He kisses Vito's hand.]

Vito: Good. Someday—and that day may never come—I'll call upon you to do a service for me. But until that day, accept this justice as a gift on my daughter's wedding day.

Bonasera: Grazie, Godfather.

Vito: Prego. [Bonasera leaves, and Vito turns to Tom.] Give this to, uh, Clemenza. I want reliable people, people who aren't going to be carried away. After all, we're not murderers, in spite of what this undertaker thinks.[38]

Bonasera has given a gift; he has made a sacrifice—they are two ways of describing the same act. He has given his fealty, his "friendship" to the godfather. In return, the godfather will give Bonasera a gift: he will dispense justice. But notice, this does not end the transaction. It merely begins it. "Someday, I'll call upon you to do a service for me." Gifts are not given, sacrifices are not made, without strings. They bind both giver and recipient with webs of ongoing mutual obligation. And those familiar with the movie know that Bonasera will indeed be called upon to do a service for the don soon. This is the economy of gift exchange that fueled the families of the ancient world, both pagan and biblical—and with a little imagination, can be seen lurking behind many practices we also take for granted.

The gospel comes to life—literally—in a world with this economy of gift exchange, and it both redeems and overturns it. We can get a sense of both by looking briefly at the weightiest "therefore" in the entire Christian Bible: "I appeal to you therefore, brothers, by the mercies of God, to present your bodies as a living sacrifice, holy and acceptable to God, which is your spiritual worship" (Rom 12:1). This "therefore" is the hinge on which the book of Romans turns. The first eleven chapters declare and explain how the righteousness of God is fully revealed in Jesus Christ. It's a righteousness that places both Jew and gentile in right standing with God, a righteousness poured into our hearts by the Holy Spirit. That's some heavy-duty theology right there. But it is heavy-duty theology put in service of a very practical question. It is not the psychological question that drove Martin Luther mad—namely, how do I, a sinner, stand before a holy God?[39] No. It is a question that is much more practical: "How do Jews and gentiles get along in one church?" And Paul's answer is both Jews and gentiles stand under God's wrath because of sin; both Jews and gentiles are placed in right standing with God through Christ and in the power of the Holy Spirit. Did Jew or gentile earn this mighty act? No! It is a gift from first to last.

So, if Jew and gentile are alike under condemnation, placed in the right by the same mighty act of God, and lay hold of that gift in the same way—namely, through faith—what difference does that make? If that's true, how should Jew and gentile together live?

Paul's answer starts in Romans 12 and continues through to the end of the book. The "therefore" signals a shift, but not from doctrine to ethics, as is often presented. It's a shift from doctrine to liturgy. Because of the gift given and received, Jews and gentiles together were to be *living* sacrifices, offering spiritual worship to God. After Christ's death on the cross, no longer would Christians smear blood on altars to cover or cleanse sins. After the ascension of Christ, no longer would Christians burn the bodies of lambs and goats to send the smoke up to God as a pleasing aroma. His death and resurrection were once for all. It brought all the previous sacrifices to their true end. The sacrifices of animals were the metaphors. The one sacrifice of Christ was the great reality to which they all pointed. The sacrifice of Christ was *the* great gift

given by God the Son on behalf of sinful humanity to God the Father to forever wash humanity's
sins and turn away his wrath in the power of God
the Spirit. *And* it was the gift of the Triune God to
us, to make us right before God when we could
do nothing to earn it. A gift to be laid hold of only
through faith. And that faith is itself a gift so that
we can boast in nothing.

Why should Jews and gentiles get along?
Because Jews and gentiles are caught up in that one
great act together. They share in the one sacrifice,
the one gift of the Son to the Father in the Spirit. In
the Spirit, they are made into the one community.
Together they are caught up in the eternal love-gift
that the Son gives to the Father. And what does that
worship look like? Just this: thinking soberly about
ourselves, recognizing the giftedness of others, out-
doing each other in works of love, extending hospitality to strangers, and on and on, all the way to
the end of the book. All of that is not ethics. It's
worship. And not just worship, but sacrificial worship. Sober self-awareness, generosity, hospitality,
love—that is what the Christian worship sacrifice
looks like. That is what the Christian gift to God
looks like. After the one sacrifice of Christ is given,

all that is left to do is continue giving. Christians will, from here on, give to God by giving to and for others.

The Triune God, who needs no gifts, indeed who cannot be bribed to be other than who he is, pours out the gift of his very life on his people that they may be bound to each other and to him forever. That is the economy of the gospel in which God, out of grace, gives the gift; out of grace, establishes ties of obligation; and out of grace, calls us to give back to him (as a living sacrifice) by emulating his giving for others to the world. It is an always-open invitation, a gift eternally given.

But can that gift be refused, not just for a time, but ultimately and forever? And what does that rejection look like? If life—this everyday life—is as I have described above, if it is a trajectory of growing closer to or more distant from the God who eternally gives himself in his Son through his Spirit for us, it seems to me that we must sadly answer, yes. A gift that cannot be refused is no gift at all. At the moment of our death, when we are confronted fully and finally by the Judge who wants only to redeem, we will not be different people than we were a moment before. We will run toward him and happiness for eternity, or we will not. Hell, in

a word, is the refusal of the gift. The judgment that
damns will be our own.

CHAPTER 5

Heaven

*There is no need to be worried by facetious people
who try to make the Christian hope of "Heaven"
ridiculous by saying they do not want "to spend
eternity playing harps."*
—C. S. Lewis

"You have to read this!" she said as she thrust the book into my hand. She was an older parishioner, not terribly pious but faithful in her church attendance. On this particular Thursday, she was in the church building for her quilting group, and she had brought me a copy of *Heaven Is for Real*. The then best-seller was the story of Colton Burpo's afterlife encounter. I confess that I took the book with a deal of skepticism and was quite surprised by what I read. There were no claims that the boy died, no outlandish visions; much of the book dealt not so much with Colton's experience as with the doubts of his father, Todd, a pastor. During emergency surgery, Colton had what began as a classic near-death experience: floating over his body while the medical team worked to save his life and seeing his father praying in the hospital chapel; this was followed by an experience of heaven in which he met his great-grandfather, a sister who had died in a miscarriage, and the Lord.[40]

Following the typical American success story, the experience became a best-selling book and a $100 million grossing movie. I don't know what Colton Burpo experienced. I've never met him or his family. I am confident that neither Colton nor his father was intentionally deceptive. But I don't think Colton went to heaven.

A different and far sadder story is Alex Malarkey's, whose own near-death experience followed a car accident that left him permanently, seriously injured.[41] Again, the basics of what followed the accident conform to classic near-death experience details: Alex left his body, was taken to heaven by an angel where he met Jesus, and came back. It was too good a story to keep quiet, and *The Boy Who Came Back From Heaven* was published by Tyndale House and soon sold over one million copies. But controversy was not far behind. Shortly after its publication, Alex and his mother claimed the story had been embellished and twisted. In early 2015, Alex publicly disavowed the book entirely, claiming he did not, in fact, go to heaven. Three years later, he initiated a lawsuit against Tyndale House, and his parents divorced.

Though the Burpo and Malarkey families' experiences are different, both testify to a hunger in our churches and in popular culture for knowledge of what awaits us after death. Both books sold well because they offered people a sense of hope for a beyond that was good. That they did so in a Christian veneer that could still resonate outside the walls of a church only helped. While there remains a market for "heaven tourism" books and videos—a quick Google search of heaven (or hell) will generate a list of far more vivid afterlife encounters than Colton Burpo's and Alex Malarkey's—these two mark a cultural turning point. Interest in the afterlife, even in secular North America, is not abating, but the explicitly Christian imagery deployed in these books is.

As I look at my watchlists on Amazon Prime and Netflix, I see *The Good Place*, *Forever*, and *Upload*, three comedies that ostensibly deal with the afterlife, and that change is clear. *The Good Place* makes the case that while the Bad Place is indeed bad, human beings can find meaning in trying to escape it; the Good Place, however, is ultimately and eventually boring; and the Best Place, ironically enough, is oblivion. It's hard not to read the show as a parable answering the question, "What follows a culture that gives us everything?" Nothing at all, it seems. *Forever* tells the story of married couple Oscar and June, who try to navigate a banal, liminal, slightly sinister afterlife both with and without each other, and neither successfully. *The Upload* is the most technologically interesting. Critically injured in a car accident, coding genius Nathan has his consciousness uploaded into a virtual afterlife known as Lakeview. It's a simulacrum of this life, with the basics provided for a flat rate and extras available for additional fees. While virtual reality and artificial intelligence even allow a certain amount of traffic between the worlds of the still embodied and the virtual—Nathan welcomes his friends to his own funeral—the sanity of the uploaded consciousnesses depends on their belief that their new world is a continuation of real life, something that persistent technical glitches prevent. There is no God in this artificial heaven, but there are therapists.

We don't need to go into the programs' details to see three contrasting takes on the afterlife. And yet, some striking commonalities serve as a starting point for this final chapter in Part I. First, every vision looks similar to this life—so much so that we could charge the screenwriters with a lack of imagination. They have rejected the fantastical accounts of the heaven tourists, but they've hardly replaced it with improvements. Second, none of the visions is terribly hopeful. Meaning is derived from trying to escape the Bad Place or stave off the banal and repetitious, or—most interestingly—finding a way of downloading consciousness back into a material body, going back to the way things were. One might even call this a perverse hope for resurrection. Their outlook is bleak. But third, the comedies can't give way to a full-blown skepticism (not least because there'd then be no script at all). For some, an indefinite continuation of life as we now know it is the new, beatific vision. And in a peculiar twist, for others, if oblivion is the ultimate answer, then it must at least be one with some sort of moral structure. It must in some way be Good, or at least better than the alternative: endless persistence.

THE INTERMEDIATE STATE

The philosopher Charles Taylor in *A Secular Age* has spoken of the secular social imaginations as "buffered." That is, we have so walled off the supernatural from the natural that any communication between the two is impossible. And that makes talking about the afterlife—if we persist in believing in it—challenging. It strikes me that the two visions described above are flipsides of the same coin, twin consequences of our strict separation. The vision of the universe in which heaven, if it exists at all, is bounded from this life by strict limits gives us an unhappy result. Either we receive a cartoon simulacrum, an extended family reunion where Jesus comes to dinner, or a slightly skewed repetition of what already is that makes the obliteration of consciousness attractive. The strict separation of heaven from earth, eternity from time, and soul from body, in other words, has robbed many of us of our ability to think about heaven in a way more consonant with the Christian Scriptures and with tradition. Regardless of what has been said about flying away when this life is o'er, Scripture and tradition affirm the resurrection of the body, and then, only after, the life everlasting. And that's where we need to begin. Heaven is about bodies.

What then about the Christian belief in the immortality of the soul affirmed in chapter 3? We must now return to that ethereal subject under a slightly different heading: the intermediate state. Let's start by recalling that the Christian understanding of the immortality of the soul grew out of the intermingling of the Platonic concern for a transcendent vision of the Good that could ground society with the Jewish conviction that the covenant faithfulness of the God of Life would not abandon the objects of his love to the grave. What cataclysmic event caused such a radical rethinking? I'll get to that in a moment.

For now, recall that the immortality of the soul is not, at its core, about disarming death by rendering the most important part of me immune from its clutches. It is about God, God's justice, and God's love. It is about God's covenant faithfulness. And as such, it cannot be dismissed as a Platonic barnacle on the pristine hull of the Authentic Ship of Biblical Faith. From this conviction grew, among some Jews in the Second Temple period, the hope that souls would one day be reunited with bodies in a perfected creation so that God's justice and love, his covenant faithfulness, would be publicly affirmed. Hence the name, "intermediate state." Wherever the blessed dead are now, they are awaiting, perhaps with even more intensity than we are, a new heaven and a new earth, with new bodies. They are waiting to enter a creation made fit for the indwelling presence of God. That is what Christians mean by heaven. And that doesn't fit very well with the hopes of the heaven tourists or the fears of the hereafter bored.

All this to say, the intermediate state truly is intermediate. Christian hope is not for life after death, as N. T. Wright is fond of saying, but life after life after death.[42] The souls of those who die in Christ remain united to him even in death, perhaps in an even stronger, more intimate union than ours. After all, to be absent from the body is to be present with the Lord (2 Cor 5:8).

Furthermore—as our Catholic brothers and sisters understand better than many of us Protestants—because the blessed dead remain united to Christ even as we do, they remain, therefore, also united to us. The point, again, is finally christological. Jesus' death did not undo the union that bound deity and humanity in the one incarnate Lord. Just so, our union with him is something death cannot sever. Because he died and is alive, he is Lord of both the dead and the living. And yet, that persistence beyond the death of the body is not the end. The hope, if we share in a death like his, is that we will share in his resurrection.

THE RESURRECTION OF THE BODY

What cataclysmic event could have so reordered the minds of the befuddled, grief-stricken disciples that they announced a new society based on the interruption of the transcendent Good into the present? What drove them to live and die on the affirmation that the present public vindication of God's covenant love had begun? The answer is found in their proclamation: "God has made him both Lord and Christ Jesus, whom you crucified" (Acts 2:36). The longed-for end—life-after-life-after-death—had broken into the present and was even now reordering things from the atoms up. Jesus was bodily alive and would never die again. If we are going to think about heaven, we need to think not about disembodied souls on clouds playing harps but about early Christian preaching. We need to think about Easter. About an empty tomb.

About a fish breakfast on the shores of Galilee. About a body.

"Make no mistake," begins John Updike's famous poem, "if he rose at all, it was as his body."[43] Updike wrote *Seven Stanzas at Easter* at a time when, on many Easter Sunday mornings, in many American pulpits, the resurrection of Jesus was metaphorized into banality, if not denied outright. By the mid-twentieth century, the Easter story had become a way of speaking about spring or reduced to a mere subjective experience—Jesus is still alive in the hearts of those who loved him. The resurrection, in other words, was not about the resurrection; it was a way of speaking about something else, something more palatable to modern minds. Never mind that the resurrection was no more palatable to ancient minds either. Everyone, both ancient and modern, knows that dead people stay that way.

Updike's poem, though often presented as a triumphalist orthodoxy, is far more circumspect. *If* there is a resurrection, he says, let it be that. To speak of it in any other way is not to find a better way to communicate to the unbelieving mind; it is to adopt the position of unbelief and so to be "crushed by cruel remonstrance."[44]

Christ's resurrection reinterpreted as spring or as a subjective encounter is, in Updike's mind, even easier to disbelieve than the real thing. And that has always been the case. Apologetic strategies that want to make Christian faith relevant, inviting, and understandable finally flounder here. If the tomb's not empty, there's no point. "*Wohlverstanden, leibliche Auferstehung,*" then, is our watchword: "Mark well, bodily resurrection."[45] Karl Barth's earnest statement to Thomas F. Torrance—two of the most important resurrection theologians of the mid-twentieth century—continues to echo.

The resurrection of Jesus was indeed a subjective experience in the minds of the disciples because it was first an objective experience in the world of Pontius Pilate. It was not simply a subjective reinterpretation of what had happened on the cross but the objective announcement of the event's meaning. The cross of Jesus really *was* a victory, a verdict, an acceptable sacrifice, and the fullest display of divine love because he who died on a Friday afternoon had appeared to Mary and to Peter and John and even, one week later, to Thomas. Here is where we begin to think about heaven because this is the fullest display of heaven on earth so far. If we want to understand heaven, then the place to start is not the imagery of Revelation—jasper walls, pearl gates, gold streets— but with the risen body of Jesus.

So what does the risen body of Jesus tell us about heaven? First of all, and running against the cultural grain, heaven is a material reality. Jesus' risen body is, for lack of a better word, hard: "Touch me, and see" (Luke 24:39); "Do not cling to me" (John 20:17). It is a body that could light a fire and cook some fish on the seashore. We are dealing here with some sort of matter. When St. Paul contrasts "spiritual" bodies from "soulish" ones (the Greek word is *psychikon*, often wrongly translated "physical") in 1 Corinthians 15:44, not only does he have the risen body of Jesus in mind, but he is extrapolating from there to consider resurrection bodies in general. He is, therefore, emphatically not contrasting immaterial souls from material bodies. Rather, it is two animating principles of two very different but equally material bodies that he has in view. Resurrection bodies, bodies that are animated by the Spirit, will be fit for a new creation, the kingdom of God; soulish bodies will not but will be "sown" (1 Cor 15:44) into the ground of the old creation. We will be raised with and into a new body, fit for a new earth in which the fullness of God will dwell.

Second, heaven is *personally* continuous with this world. That is to say, in heaven, we will be the people we were before we died. The Easter message, straightforwardly, is this: he who was crucified on Friday afternoon was alive again Sunday morning; we saw him. It was the *same* person, transformed. This is perhaps the most significant implication of Thomas' encounter with the risen Lord. He does not doubt that the ten have seen … someone. He wants to know that that someone is the very one who died. "Unless I … place my finger into the mark of the nails … I will never believe" (John 20:25). And Jesus obliges: "Put your finger here" (John 20:27).

The Emmaus Road encounter is especially instructive here. Cleopas and his companion, to be sure, did not recognize the risen Jesus, but *not* because Jesus had changed. It was rather because their normal powers of perception were inhibited. "Their eyes were held," says St. Luke (24:16, author's translation). The Easter Jesus was, in the words of the ascension angel, "This same Jesus" (Acts 1:11 NIV). Let's unpack that a little more.

My Dad, when he mused about heaven, asked more than once, "Will I still be fat?" I don't know that he wanted to have Brad Pitt's body in heaven, but he had always been on the heavier side and hoped, in the resurrection, that he would be found somewhat slimmer. It's silly, I know, but behind the self-conscious joke, there is a substantial question: Will the quirks and foibles and even sins that in some way make us, us, persist in heaven?

Let me put it less flippantly. A friend of mine has been paralyzed for over twenty years because of a camping accident. I have heard him say more than once that he's not sure if he wants to be healed in the usual way we think of healing. His paralysis is so much a part of him that suddenly having two working legs would in some way undo the person he's become since his accident. He would not be recognizable to himself.

I think the answer to my dad's question and my friend's worry is the same. Christ's risen body still bears the wounds we inflicted. They continue to make and disclose him as he really is. But they are no longer sources of pain and suffering. They are "rich wounds yet visible above, in beauty glorified."[46] If that's true of the Lord's raised humanity, then that implies the experiences that make us who we are, including even the negative ones, are not entirely undone in the resurrection. They will not be erased; they will be transformed such that every tear they once inspired will be wiped away.

Continuity, however, is only half the story. There is, third, discontinuity as well. Even if the risen Christ could be touched, he was not limited by the physical laws that constrain us. He could appear in a locked room (John 20:19). Likewise, he could disappear at will (Luke 24:31). The question is how to frame the discontinuity. It cannot be framed in terms of identity. It is the same person as before. On Sunday morning, Jesus is not other than who he was on Friday afternoon. It cannot be framed spatially. Heaven is not a place entirely other than earth if the body of Jesus can traffic between the two. The risen Jesus is, in his transformed humanity, even more himself. He is the first glimpse of a creation made fit for the dwelling of God.

THE LIFE EVERLASTING

Heaven, then, is about a new creation, or better, a renewing of creation—and that's why the strict separation of heaven and earth that has dominated the Western imagination for nearly 300 years won't do. So what do we do? We begin, as we have done, with the resurrection of Jesus, and then we reimagine the whole of creation in that light, and that means not fanciful forays or despairing dreams but turning again to the Old Testament, to which the resurrection of Jesus provides a radical hermeneutical key. Tracing an Old Testament theology of heaven is well beyond the scope of this short work. But following N. T. Wright in his book *History and Eschatology*, we can touch on three signposts, which will give us a sense of direction: temple, Sabbath, and humans as image.

The tabernacle at first and then the temple afterward were microcosms of the universe. Their architecture made clear that they were to be understood as the whole world, at the center of which was God's dwelling place. They were signs that pointed both back to the primordial goodness of God's creation and ahead to the future hope that one day God would inhabit his home again. The temple was a sign pointing to a creation made by God for God: a home in which he could rest. Which brings us next to Sabbath. When Jesus heals and proclaims himself Lord of the Sabbath (Matt 12:1–8; Mark 2:23–28; Luke 6:1–5), he is not liberalizing against the legalistic Pharisees. He is disclosing the Sabbath's true meaning. If God had returned to his creation, then all that enslaves that creation—sin, death, and the devil—is banished by the presence of Life. How, then, can he not heal on the Sabbath? There is no better day to give life than on the day God returns to claim what is his own. Creation today longs for the true Sabbath rest of the people of God, the day in which death will be forever banished and Life given to the full. Human beings, finally, are created and called by their Creator to be his images in his temple and priests on his Sabbath day.

It would be tempting here to shift our gaze away from the risen Jesus to the new creation that his resurrection foreshadows, that awaits its full unveiling at his appearance. But to do so would be a mistake. To do so would only be a more sophisticated way of turning heaven into a family reunion rather than a union with the Lord. We do need to say more, including about the community of the blessed dead. But we cannot move from the signposts straight to heaven, for temple, Sabbath, and humans as image find their completion not so much in heaven, as in Jesus. As the writer to the Hebrews makes plain in his commentary on Psalm 8 (Heb 2:5–9), we do not yet see any of this! But we do see Jesus who, in his person, *is* God returned to his creation, who is the cornerstone of the new temple. We see Jesus, who, in his person, extends to all the invitation to enter into the true Sabbath rest of God. We see Jesus, who is the image of the invisible God, the recoverer of humanity's true vocation, who is both fully God and fully human—indeed, whose humanity is so much more than ours is at present. To talk about heaven (before the parousia and the new creation, at least) is ultimately to talk about Jesus: "Christ is the temple of the final age; he is heaven, the new Jerusalem; he is the cultic space for God. The ascending movement of humanity in its union with Christ is answered by the descending movement of God's love in its self-gift to us."[47] Heaven, then, is the perfection of the church's and the believer's union with Christ, which is already (imperfectly) true. It is nothing less and nothing other than the removal of every obstacle to the whole and perfect worship of God the Father in the power of the Spirit.

Only now, keeping our eyes fixed on Jesus, can we speak of what Ratzinger calls the ecclesiological and cosmological dimensions of heaven.[48] My going to heaven is both dependent upon and, in some way, equated with my being in Christ. And this involves, necessarily, a union with all others who are likewise a part of his body, his bride, his church. If heaven is the removal of every impediment to my full communion with God, it is also consequently the removal of every impediment to my full communion with his children, my brothers and sisters. The cycle of self-giving, which we spoke of in the previous chapter, here finds its fullest expression. The joy of heaven will never become boring because we will always be giving of ourselves to God by giving to each other from his inexhaustible riches. As Reepicheep, the buccaneering mouse of the Narnia chronicles, rightly insists, there will always be "further up and further in" to Aslan's country.[49]

And this brings us finally to the place where the tourists and comedians want to begin—the cosmology of heaven. If heaven is, as I have tried to describe it, the exaltation of humanity into the life of God, an exaltation foreshadowed and guaranteed by the resurrection and ascension of Jesus, then heaven is not a spatial reality. Heaven is not an as-yet undetected planet X, whether in our or some other solar system. Indeed, heaven is already an imperfectly experienced reality for those who are in Christ, all who are at this moment members of the church militant and the church triumphant.

That for which we wait is not a space, but a time—the time in which all reality is drawn into the presence of God. The time in which our bodies are transformed by the Spirit in order to live forever in that new creation. On that day, we will not so much be *in* heaven as we will *be* heaven, and God will be all and in all.

Part II

Pastoral Practice

CHAPTER 6

Catechist

The bodies of the newly dead are not debris nor remnant, nor are they entirely icon or essence. They are, rather, changelings, incubates, hatchlings of a new reality that bear our names and dates, our image and likenesses, as surely in the eyes and ears of our children and grandchildren as did word of our birth in the ears of our parents and their parents. It is wise to treat such new things tenderly, carefully, with honor.
—Thomas Lynch

Until now, we've been dealing in the realm of theological theory. It's now time to try to put that theory into practice: What should sojourning with a family in the valley of the shadow of death look like if what we've said in the previous chapters is true?

I'll sketch an answer to that question over the next four chapters, dealing with the initial meeting with the family, followed by the funeral service, the sermon, and finally aftercare. Every case you encounter will, of course, be unique, and I will necessarily remain at a general level as a result. Nonetheless, my goal in Part II is straightforward: to convince you that you will comfort, worship, proclaim, and love as a pastor. You're there to do soul-work that no one else can do. You are not a poorly paid social worker, therapist, or funeral director. As important as these other vocations are—I certainly don't disparage them—the pastoral role is important, too. The church provides an essential service, in itself independent from those acts in which it might overlap with other institutions. Just so, even if pastors provide for family needs or offer therapeutic or practical funerary advice, you are essential workers in yourselves, performing those tasks that only you can. And not simply because of your skills and training. It is because of your vocation—your call and commission by God as recognized by God's people to be a shepherd of souls. You do not need to justify your work by imitating the work of others or trying to translate it into another professional vocabulary. As John Piper is fond of saying, you are not a professional.[50]

These next chapters will describe those unique aspects of pastoral work in caring for a grieving family. When you meet with a family, of course, you are a pastor—you are one throughout. You are there to offer comfort, in the old English sense of strengthening and not merely soothing. But at some point, the meeting with the family will move to nuts and bolts about the funeral service. What Scriptures will be read? What songs, sung? Who will pray and eulogize? Those are practical questions to be sure, but they are not merely practical. Through the conversation that they spur along, you are teaching your family the Christian way of death in the most intense classroom they will ever have. You are a pastor, yes, and here your primary role is that of catechist.

THE DEATH OF THE FUNERAL?

It might seem counterproductive to begin by saying you—the pastor—are not needed for a funeral. This is not simply down to the rapidly changing cultural mores of late modernity, either.

The gunslingers Chris and Vin meet for the first time at a clergy-less funeral in *The Magnificent Seven* (the original movie from 1960, not the 2016 remake). Paid by a traveling salesman to transport the body of a local man from the town square to the cemetery against the wishes of the townspeople, Vin rides shotgun while Chris manages to drive the hearse to the burial ground, where they persuade six reluctant locals to act as pallbearers.

It may seem like an extreme situation, but it makes my point. When you strip away all the ritual actions associated with the disposal of the dead, a funeral is simply about moving a body from one place to another. And a pastor is not needed for that (neither, for that matter, is a social worker, therapist, or funeral director). All that's really needed is a body and someone to move it. In this sense, the funeral is an act as old as humanity. In fact, some anthropologists date the emergence of humanity on an evolutionary scale with the emergence of funerary rites. Some animals—primates or elephants, for example, and even crows—seem to mourn their dead; only humans display their mourning by cleaning, visiting, and disposing of the body. Funerals are deeply and profoundly human.

Until now. Gone are the elaborate mourning rituals of the Victorian era, which plotted the mourning time into three stages—full mourning, second mourning, and half-mourning. Along with those divisions, mourning periods were specified: two years for widows, one year for children whose parents had died, and decreasing with familial distance from the deceased. Mourning, and the stages thereof, was publicly signaled by the way mourners dressed. To breach the rule was to dishonor the dead[51]—especially for women, whose rules for appropriate dress and demeanor were far more strict and elaborate than those for men. A young widow, especially if she was attractive, would be suspected not simply of frivolity, but sexual promiscuity, if she signaled a premature end to her mourning period of one to two years by wearing something brightly colored or attending a celebration such as a wedding.

Today, by contrast, almost anything goes. Traditional funerals continue to take place, but they are increasingly replaced by various sorts of celebrations from which displays of grief are as oddly absent as the deceased himself. Not long ago, I was asked to officiate at the funeral of a man I did not know. I had come recommended to the family by the local funeral director. When I called the family to arrange a meeting, it was apparent that a miscommunication had taken place. Faith of any sort was not a central part of this family's life. When I asked about Scripture readings, they were reluctant. When I brought up the subject of prayer, they were very uncomfortable. Finally, I said to them, "When I deal with families I don't know, it's usually because they're looking for a Christian clergyman. And that means we'll have at least that in common to build from. I don't know your family, and I'm pretty sure you don't want Christian content in your service. Is that right?" That question allowed us to get to the heart of the matter. They weren't interested in a Christian funeral at all, and ultimately I couldn't help them. People are going to die; what happens afterward is up for grabs.

Thomas Lynch and Thomas Long, in their important book *The Good Funeral*, lament the loss of the funeral as a cultural act in late modernity. At bottom, they argue, is modernity's profound discomfort with the bodily reality of death. We have, perhaps thankfully, moved away from the rigid social script of the Victorian way of death. But we've not replaced it with anything else, or perhaps better, we've replaced it with everything else.

Long and Lynch think (and I'm inclined to agree) that part of this movement reflects our cultural discomfort with death and specifically with bodies. We don't talk about death anymore; and so when it happens, we need to move past it as quickly as possible. Lynch and Long see this dynamic at work in how we have chosen to avoid dealing with a body.

Consider, for instance, the growth in cremation in North America. Cremations now represent 53 percent of disposals in the United States. And that number is only going to rise; in urban centers, it is already well above that. In my small town in Quebec, Canada, cremations represent 80 percent of the local funeral director's cases. The problem is not cremation per se, but how it is done in North America. For example, in the United Kingdom, where cremation has had a more extended period of social acceptance, the family processes with the body to the crematorium as part of the funeral rite. In other cultures (and other faiths), disposal by burning is the accepted norm and part of elaborate funerary rituals. By contrast, cremation in North America has largely arisen as a cost-saving device and a means of expediting the disposition of the body. Often, the last time the family sees the body is when it is removed from the place of death. The bodily means by which families would come psychologically to deal with death—washing, dressing, and laying out the body, welcoming visitors for the viewing, eating together, the funeral, and the burial—are severely attenuated or eliminated altogether. In its place, the family makes a phone call and, sometimes just a few hours later, arrives at the funeral home to pick up a box of remains. Everything else—an urn, a wake, a funeral, or nothing at all—is up to them. They are customers; the funeral director has products to sell them.

None of the funeral directors I've spoken with about the consumerization of death are happy about it. While I've read several articles written by directors who seem enthusiastic to embrace and drive the change, the reaction I greet in person is always resignation tinged with sadness: "I try to tell them they need to do something, but they think I'm just out to get their money." Having worked in a funeral home and seen good people try to help grieving families and make a living doing so, I have not only heard this sentence, I've seen the stress that underlies it. Long and Lynch believe that the consumerization of the funeral is psychologically and spiritually harmful. It forecloses on the means human beings need to deal with grief.[52]

For thousands of years, funerals have involved a body, a family who cares for it, and a ritualized movement of a body from the community of the living to the community of the dead, there to take up its new residence. Through that movement, the living themselves come to the very threshold of that other, larger community, and there they grieved their losses, shared them in the wider group, and confronted questions of mortality, transcendence, and what comes after.

Funerals, in short, provide the concrete space and literal language to permit people to make sense of a limit- and language-shattering experience. They help people. In a consumerized industry— where churches are more and more often politely passed over—chapels are transformed into celebration centers, and pastors and officiants into celebration planners—it is difficult to see how the work that needs to be done *can* be done. In her memoir of her mother's death, Megan O'Rourke speaks of being relieved to have everything looked after when her mother died. It was all done quickly, efficiently, and out of sight. Later, however, she noticed how the suspension of her mourning at the time made her grieving longer and more difficult. "I wonder," she mused after seeing her mother's ashes in a simple box on her father's nightstand one year later, "if it might have helped me to take care one last time of the body I'd cared about my entire life."[53]

The Practicalities

This is the reality into which you have been thrown and the reality you have to work against for the family's sake. The nuts-and-bolts conversation that must happen is placed in a different, more serious context when you realize this. Whether you meet the family in the hospital or hospice, the funeral home, their home, the church office, or a coffee shop, this is your reality. Whether your family is churched, unchurched, or dechurched, this is your reality. It is your reality because it is theirs. And it is your task to lovingly take a sledgehammer to it. Humans have learned over thousands of years of cultural evolution to grieve (a mental, spiritual process) with a body (a physical reality) and with rites peculiar to its disposal (the funeral). Today, we've removed the bodies and turned the rites into a cafeteria of options, many of which are casual, trite, and sometimes just plain silly. No wonder why, as a culture, we are so psychologically slapdash when it comes to grieving. Your job as a pastor is to try to teach your family out of this frame of mind *for their own soul's sake*. And it begins with the practicalities.

Up against this near monumental task are the practical constraints. If the family you're shepherding is churched—one of yours—you may well be ahead of the game, if teaching the Christian way of death has come up as a regular part of your parish life. If you're like me, however, that's not been high on the priority list of programs, Bible studies, sermon series, and so on. Even the most churched of families these days is more gnostic than Christian when it comes to death. They easily move in the consumer model because they've absorbed the notion that bodies don't matter; the soul has gone to heaven.

When you're meeting the family for the first time, and all you have is the one or two hours they can give you before the funeral, your situation is even worse. Your family may well say something like, "What made Dad, Dad, is gone. We can do with the body what we want." Their outlook is not gnostic (betting on a deathless soul) but fully epicurean (there is no soul). Consciousness is merely a function of the brain, and when the brain no longer functions, consciousness ends. All the more reason to simply discard the body. That's the classroom dynamic when it comes time to teach the Christian way of death. And yet, even if you only have one hour in a coffee shop, that family has chosen you (perhaps the one upside of the consumer model), and that means there's a chink in their armor ready-made for the Holy Spirit to enlarge through you.

Your meeting with the family will transition through three moments. You'll begin by discerning their need. Here the most basic questions need to be considered. Is the family churched, dechurched, or unchurched? The most straightforward meetings unfold when the family is churched and is active in your sphere of ministry. Hopefully, there will already be a good rapport established. Sometimes the family will be churched, but, for any number of reasons, you rather than their regular pastor will be called upon to help. Establishing a rapport needs to take place here, but again, it should happen naturally. A churched family will hopefully have an intuitive sense of the place and purpose of Christian faith in caring for the bereaved and the dead. They will have an orientation of trust toward you as clergy, even if they've only just met you, and will therefore be open to your pastoral work. You won't need to break up their fallow ground before the seed of the gospel can be sown.

At the other end of the spectrum, your family may be dechurched. Instead of rapport, awareness, and trust, you may well find tension, resistance, and suspicion, particularly if the dechurching is recent. In my experience, unchurched families— who will come to you on the recommendation of the funeral director or to honor the deceased's faith that they do not share—simply don't know what they don't know. You might not have an established rapport with them, but you won't be meeting with resistance either. Perhaps the biggest challenge here is one of time. Dechurched and unchurched families are more likely to get to the basics and want to move on fairly quickly, yet these are the very ones where more time ought to be invested. If time permits, try to have two meetings with these families—one to build rapport and trust by learn-ing about the deceased and another to plan the service. In between, it might be wise to leave them a service outline so that they can become more familiar with it.

Is the family's loss tragic or merely sad? All deaths are sad; not all are tragic. The death of a child or young person, a suicide (whether or not a medically assisted one), a sudden death—these are tragic. And all represent unique challenges in your initial meeting with the family. You will enter into each situation differently, and, I'm sad to say, the only way to become aware of the dynamics unique to tragic deaths is to experience them. I'm often tempted in these situations to speak too much, whether to the family or to God in prayer on their behalf. I have found that silence and letting them lead, at least at first, is necessary. Observing raw, intense grief can be a discomfiting experience, and such grief may well exacerbate already complicated family dynamics, heightening your uneasiness even more.

In such cases, you will need to resist the urge to dissociate from the situation or tune out, in order to be as immediately and fully present as possible to your family. In such situations, the reality of your ordination may offer a helpful reminder: you are in that situation as a representative of Christ and his church. That is your job. This ought not to add to the sense of being overwhelmed, but hopefully it will ease your burden. You can't fix this problem, so don't try. Just be there, and be there *as Christ* in *the power of the Holy Spirit.*

And of course, concrete needs must be considered, and many families today cannot afford even a simple funeral. Costs vary regionally, but not much. In my area, a basic traditional funeral will cost around $5,000. And spending twice that amount is possible without moving much further toward the more elaborate end of the scale. If you are going to suggest that a more traditional funeral, with a casket or an urn present, will be a long-term benefit to your family emotionally and spiritually, you may need to be prepared to offer concrete support. If your family is poor or has no church connection, will your parish provide support? Will you offer your church building for free? Will your social organizers prepare a lunch at a reduced rate or even gratis? Has your church set aside a fund to help poorer families with funeral costs? Money is a sensitive topic, and you will need to broach it carefully. Often a quiet word with the funeral director—who more than likely has already met with them—will clarify how you ought to proceed.

The second moment in meeting the family will arise when the concrete issues, such as money, do. At this point, you will have to disabuse their assumptions about what is happening. Even the most churched family will enter the conversation from the assumption that they are consumers, and you are a service provider. This assumption is false, and perniciously so. You are providing soul-care that is every bit as real as a medical doctor's care for a human body. That a patient pays her doctor does not permit her to dictate what her treatment ought to be. Certainly people are free to decline your services, as did the family I mentioned at the outset of this chapter. But once they have entered the pastoral relationship with you, shift them out of this consumer mindset as gently but as firmly as you can.

Another assumption that will need to be challenged, this time more indirectly, is that their loved one's wishes ought always to be incorporated. Beloved Scripture readings, songs, favorite stories can, of course, be considered and included when planning the service. But as the next section and chapter will explore more fully, the deceased is not the center of the funeral service. As a service of Christian worship, God is. We offer the Father our grief-soaked sacrifice of praise in the name of the Son and the power of the Spirit to bring this liminal human experience into the fullness of the divine life and love. More practically, the first commandment is to have no other gods before God (the

Bible points this out from Genesis to Revelation, the classic text being Romans 1:18–32). To break that commandment doesn't hurt God's "feelings" as much as it brings harm to those who have been created in God's image—human beings. This is no less true at a funeral, and it is your starting point for planning—even if it is not the family's. It is also quite possible that, out of love and a deep desire to honor their loved one, a family will feel constrained by last wishes that are neither wise nor helpful and may hear "not all wishes can or should be accommodated" as words of liberation.

The third moment in your conversation is the actual description of the service. As you seek input from the family where appropriate, take care to remember that this is a worship service that aims always at the glorification of God by centering on Christ crucified and risen. A good funeral will accomplish three tasks. First, it will commit the deceased to the care of God. The family's loved one is dead. Not passed away. Not moved to the other room. Not always with them. A funeral is, in part, the provision of a context in which that hard truth need not be a soul-shattering one. The good news of the gospel is that while death sunders even the most intimate of human bonds, it does not sunder the believer's union with Christ in God, which alone guarantees our eventual reunion with them. The loved one is not lost to God. Of course, real life is complicated, and in situations where such complications cloud a straightforward announcement such as this, it is always right and proper to affirm that, like Christ's wounds, the deceased's full life and self—their virtues, vices, complications, and compromises—are brought before the face of God. He alone will judge, and will do so rightly, fully, and finally.

A good funeral will also comfort the bereaved with the grace of God. Hope is found not in the deceased's relative piety or morality, still less in the cloying sentimentality that portrays heaven as a happier continuation of the present. Hope is found in the one who has freely determined for all eternity not to be God without us, and sent his Son to reconcile us and his Spirit to unite us to him. Only as the reality of death is brought ritually and therefore really within the love of God can Christian hope be found.

Lastly, a good funeral will call the living to repentance in the context of judgment and hope in the love of God. The call to repentance is not unique to the funeral; it is part of every service of the Word (or should be), not least because people need to hear that their sins confessed really are forgiven. Many have heard horror stories of preachers taking advantage of a funeral sermon to "scare the hell" out of the living by rehearsing the torments of the recently departed. That is not what I mean. The classic text here is Hebrews 9:27–28, where the reality of death and judgment are straightforwardly announced in the larger frame of expectant hope in the final appearing of the Savior. A gospel call to repentance, to sober reflection and a change of life—especially at a funeral—should be able to conclude by singing with Charles Wesley, "Rejoice in glorious hope! Our Lord and judge shall come and take His servants up to their eternal home."[54] Sobriety and joy are not mutually exclusive. Both need to be present, especially here.

Because every family is different and every death especially so, what I have written here is six inches above lived experience. In reality, you can't leave it at this level, lest your funeral practice seem less than human. As much as I would like, especially for younger colleagues in ministry, I cannot provide detailed case studies to address every application question in advance. You'll need to write your own. If you are blessed to know or work alongside an old hand at the theologically and biblically rich fully pastoral encounter—I have found stiff Westminster Calvinists and equally unrelenting Catechism Catholics to be the most helpful to me—apprentice yourself to them! Write out your cases to review with them. A master will show you how to apply appropriate funeral theology and sometimes do so even without realizing that's what they're doing.

JIM

"Daddy, I don't understand what she's saying," my daughter said as she handed me the phone one Saturday morning. The first words I heard on the other end were, "It's Jim. He's dead." I was new to the parish, but I had already met Jim, his wife Pat, and two of their daughters and their families. Jim had brought a pie to the parish office my first day there. "This is from us," he said. I soon learned that this simple act of kindness was a major accomplishment for Jim, whose dementia was beginning to worsen. Jim and Pat had been pillars in the parish for many years. They had raised their family there after emigrating from Ireland. And being Irish, they had an ingrained sense of the place of faith and church in a well-ordered life—so much so that, when Jim died, Pat called the priest before she called the funeral director, a time-honored but rarely practiced arrangement. I jotted down some details and headed to the hospital to meet with Pat and her children. When I arrived, I was shown into the emergency room by a nurse. And there were Pat and her daughters. And Jim.

By this time in my ministry, I had planned several funerals either in my church office or at the family home. Now was the first time to do so in the presence of the dead. With Jim in the room, we shared stories, talked about hymns and eulogies and prayers, and discussed the wake before (this was an Irish family, after all) and the reception after. The details were ironed out later at the church, but we started planning for Jim's last journey with Jim (himself and yet not) in the middle of the room. This event sticks out as the paradigm of how a funeral ought to be planned. Even if it only rarely (if ever) takes place, a wise pastor will remember to meet the family in the presence of the dead to plan a movement from the community of the living to the community of the dead. The deceased is the most vulnerable person in the room—who can do nothing anymore and whose mortal remains are completely in the hands of others. The family of the deceased are those who will traverse with their loved one to the very threshold of the community of the dead, where they will leave their loved one and then make the journey back to the land of the living.

You will help your family pick the hymns, assign the tasks of praying and eulogizing, and prepare the services. Gleaning the essential information you need to prepare the service will take approximately twenty minutes. But if that's all you're doing, you are about as much pastoral help as Chris and Vin—the job will get done, you'll get paid, and that will be all. You are much more than emcee or even an officiant. You are a catechist, teaching a family not simply the rites and rules of the Christian funeral, but the substance of the gospel in the midst of death. You are teaching the Christian way to die.

CHAPTER 7

Liturgist

Death is a private affair. A funeral is a public occasion. Grief is borne by the immediate family and close friends, that little band of bereaved clustered around the remains. The funeral provides the liturgy where, for a brief interval, grief can be contained while the final separation takes place. It employs a language, chiseled out over centuries, to comfort the grief-stricken where ordinary words fail. Ritual, mercifully, accommodates private grief and public sympathy.
—Liam Swords

WORDS MATTER. I GREW UP WITH A LOVE OF them, having been surrounded by books for as long as I can remember. In the books I read as a child, words had the power to change things. "Speak 'friend' and enter," inscribed on the gates to the Mines of Moria, was the riddle that confounded the Company of the Ring until Gandalf the Wizard remembered that it was written in a simpler time. Laughing, he spoke the Elvish word for friend, "*mellon*," and the gates to the great city beneath the mountains opened. Later, when I read to my children, they learned about the "Deplorable Word," which, when uttered, destroyed Queen Jadis's world of Charn.[55] They tried to guess that word, much to their mother's embarrassment and my delight, but since our world is still here, they clearly didn't guess correctly. When they could read on their own, they learned that "Occulus Reparo" could fix a pair of broken glasses,[56] and "Wingardium Leviosa" could levitate a feather.[57] They discovered that some words were so harmful to others they could never ever be uttered. That last lesson is an especially powerful one for all of us. Words change reality. Some words still have magical powers.

Of course, one need not believe in "magic"— whether J. R. R. Tolkien's, C. S. Lewis's, or J. K. Rowling's version—to see the plainness of the point. Your name, signed by you at the bottom of a bunch of words, can finalize the purchase of a car, secure a place to live, and guarantee a specific course of action. When you were married, you were not married by a judge or a preacher or even God. Like the invitees to your wedding, they were witnesses to something you and your spouse did by speaking words. Before you made your vows, you were engaged. Afterward, you were married. Those words were performative. Without magic wands or gestures, symbol or ritual, they changed your status in law *and* in reality. Even in the everyday world where people are born, marry, live, and die, words have transformative power. And for that reason, words matter.

Words matter at funerals because a funeral is a liminal experience. You are bringing a family to the thin place where two realities intersect. One perfectly natural and appropriate way to speak of those realities—the communities of the living and the dead—has already made an appearance in this book. Another way, using perhaps even more important language for this transition (at least for believers), is this: the church militant and the church triumphant. At the conclusion of the funeral of my best friend's father, a local pastor stood in the midst of the congregation and announced, "I move that we strike Ray's name from the membership roll. He has taken his membership to another, bigger congregation." The motion was seconded and passed unanimously. Words are the means by which we bring this liminal experience into our shared reality. Words help us journey with the dead to their new community and then bring us back again to the land of the living.

Words break, of course, at this experience. By this I mean, they can't do what we want them to do in everyday language. The reason is simple: none of us ever having been dead can describe what being dead is like. We can speak eloquently and importantly, and both literally and concretely about the process of dying. But there are no words for being dead. Our collective fascination with ghosts and reports of near-death experiences and tours of heaven by the recently returned is at bottom a reluctance to admit that some doors admit only in one direction.

So we are left with metaphor, for metaphors are how we stretch language to pull the indescribable into the realm of description. The "community of the dead" is one such metaphor and a very helpful one, I think. The "church triumphant" is another. Both of them are true; both are inadequate to the task of full description. The turn to metaphor does not mean, however, that words do not matter, that anything goes, that we should swap out the language of heaven and hell for "The Great Golf Course in the Sky." A turn to metaphor, if anything, means that the words have to be chosen even more carefully, scripted even more tightly, lest we lapse into soft sentimentality that provides only momentary relief at the cost of no longer telling the truth. The metaphors with which we speak of death ought not to be about emotional evocation but *true if inadequate* description.

In this chapter, we'll turn to the funeral service proper, and to your pastoral role as liturgist: the one who will craft the words by which the family in your care will make the journey to the bottom of the valley of the shadow of death. Your words will equip them to go there, and there find Jesus, who, because he died and rose again, is Lord of both the living and the dead. Your words will provide the language through which they will express their grief to God, their friends, and themselves. Your words will open their eyes to gospel hope. Your words will matter. And as any old hand at the pastoral plow will tell you, death will have turned the ground of many hearts over, opening them to the seed of the Word in your words like no other experience. I can't tell you how many pastors have said to me, "I'd rather preach at a funeral than at a wedding. I know they're listening!" All this to say, you owe it to the God who called you, the church that ordained you, and the family in your care to choose your words with care. You are a liturgist.

AN ALLERGY TO LITURGY?

That is likely not a welcome announcement for many. Liturgists are picayune people arguing over vestments, church year colors, and the most appropriate preposition for this or that prayer. And liturgy means the life scripted out of the service, with no room for surprise, spontaneity, or the Holy Spirit.

I have seen this worry at work from the two ends of the liturgical spectrum. I grew up in a free church tradition, the Wesleyan Church, which celebrates its revivalist and pietist heritage. I serve in that denomination now. In this branch of Christ's church, "They read their prayers!" is a dig, an indication of spiritual deficiency. Earlier in this century, in at least one segment of the church, pulpits were suspect because pulpits meant the preacher needed something more than the Bible and the Spirit to get the job done. For many years between my childhood and now, I served as an

Anglican priest and liturgically still find my home in the Book of Common Prayer. At the evangelical end of this denomination, many share my free church friends' worries, even if they don't state them as bluntly. On the liberal end, the objection doesn't disappear as much as it takes on a different hue. Here, a focus on liturgy gets in the way of doing justice. Worship, for my liberal friends, seems at times almost ancillary to the church's true mission, which is to baptize, bless, and boost the latest item on the progressive social agenda.

Undoubtedly, some of you have personal experiences that justify these sorts of objections; others may think them largely overblown. I don't want to enter that argument; it is one of those endless, fruitless disputes common in churches. I do want to acknowledge that even if they are sometimes overdone, these sorts of worries do gesture to something true. But that truth—namely, that worship can prevent an authentic encounter with God as easily as it can engender it—is not limited to those of us who find written prayers an aid in corporate worship. I can recall a layman in my church whose Sunday morning prayers always began with, "Our dear heavenly Father." One need not be a prayer-book Christian to have heard, "Lead, guide, and direct," or to have asked for "journeying mercies." Every church has a liturgical memory that is made present every Sunday morning, even if that memory is not, has never been, nor will ever be written down. Every liturgy, written or not, can lead us to the threshold of heaven; each one can deafen us to the Lord knocking at the outside of our assembly.

Nevertheless, the funeral is one of at least two Christian services where everything, as much as possible, ought to be scripted. The other one is the wedding. Like funerals, weddings have become entirely consumerized affairs where every item and aspect boil down to the couple's desires. In a church or at the beach? A judge, a minister or rabbi, a family friend with a temporary license? Traditional or personalized vows? It's all up to you. Marriage has been reduced to the wedding. And the wedding is nothing more than the public declaration and celebration (and perhaps sanctification) of one couple's sexual desire. And if that's all it is, we really should just make it up as we go. Except, the traditional language reminds us that after the wedding comes the marriage, and marriage will hopefully last "for better or worse, for richer or poorer, in sickness and in health, until death parts us." It is an institution bigger than the couple, bigger than their erotic desire for each other, which is necessarily fleeting. The couple, and those who witness their vows, need to be reminded of that. This is why we ought not to tinker with the promises that do the work of marrying one to another.

A similar dynamic holds with the funeral. When we fiddle with the language that has been refined through centuries to enable us to express our mourning, commit our loved ones to God's merciful judgment and holy love, and find hope in the resurrection of Jesus, we end up harming not only the decorum of the event, but infinitely more importantly, the souls of those who need such hope. Death is bigger than one family's experience of grief. And it deserves a bigger acknowledgment than a retirement roast with a few prayers thrown in. The resurrection of Jesus and the hope of heaven is so much more than the sentimentalized, trite imagery that we spoke of in chapter 5. It is better to prepare your family, as much as you can, for the words that cannot change without cost than to alter the formula for the sake of people's feelings. Just as Harry, Hermione, and Ron—the Golden Trio of characters in the Harry Potter series—struggled to get the words just right so that the magic would work, so should you when preparing a funeral. Whether you are scripting it or someone else scripts it for you, show appropriate care in what you say, because the souls of your family need the salve only those words can provide.

Eulogies, Scriptures, and Hymns

Even if the service's focus is not the deceased, they are the second-most important person, though they are not, in fact, in the room. The choices we spoke of in the previous chapter need to be made, and it is best if they are made in consultation with the family. Many families, especially those who are unchurched or have been dechurched, will in the first instance want to defer to you. After all, you are the religious expert, and they are unfamiliar, uncomfortable, and even unwilling to engage in these sorts of conversations. Nevertheless, as much as possible, you do need to engage them, for in so doing, you'll come to know them and the deceased better, and this will inform your homily or sermon. I'll take the sermon up in the next chapter. For now, I want to focus on eulogies, Scriptures, and hymns.

The eulogy is without a doubt the riskiest moment of the service, especially if, like me, you've become convinced of the importance of words and of the liturgy as a finely tuned, powerful instrument of pastoral care. The reason is obvious: the eulogy is outside your control.

My most disastrous experience with a eulogy came early on in my experience of parish ministry. A son came to the pulpit to eulogize his father. Right away, I noticed he had no notes, and my first thought was, "Uh oh. This is going to be either thirty seconds or thirty minutes." Forty-five minutes later, when he finally sat down, the service almost had to be restarted. The issue was not time—though it *was* excessive—but focus. Just who was the center of the service? In this case, the focus on God, and on Bill as God's child given back to God, was lost. Nothing the son said was inappropriate to the setting; however, God was slowly pushed out of the consciousness of the congregation, and the purpose of the service was lost.

Having heard the embarrassments other priests and ministers have had to sit through with grieving families, I count myself lucky. I don't know a minister who doesn't cringe at stories that begin with the words, "I'm sorry Father (or Pastor), but ..."

And I don't doubt that many readers can top the tale I just told. They are the war stories of clergy retreats. Perhaps a better move then is to not have a eulogy at all. That certainly is one option—one taken, for example, by the Catholic Church, which in 1989 included these words in its Revised Order of Christian Funerals: "A brief homily based on the readings should always be given at the funeral liturgy, but never any kind of eulogy." In my experience, however, a eulogy is worth the risk for the following reasons.

First, it frees you from having to "know" the deceased. While there will certainly be cases where you did know the deceased well enough to write a eulogy yourself, there will be many more where you do not. And there is something disingenuous about relating stories told to you by the family, even if the weakest of connections to the deceased is common knowledge in the room. Second, and related, it frees you in the sermon to focus on the proclamation of the Word. The temptation in a eulogy-less funeral is to turn the sermon into a eulogy, which I have seen happen even in Catholic funerals. But they are two different events, aimed at two different goals. If a eulogy is done well by a friend or family member, you are free to do what you do well: situate those stories within the context of the good news of a crucified and risen Lord. Third, it allows the family to bring their grief personally and directly into the context of worship—which is, of course, what a funeral ought to be about in its entirety. If the imprecatory Psalms are intended for a worship context, then a eulogy can function well in one, too.

So despite a couple of wince-worthy experiences, I have come to believe that the pastoral power of a good eulogy is worth the liturgical risk. Nevertheless, going this route does require a bit more planning, especially in the cases of unchurched or dechurched families. If there is to be a eulogy, sit down with the eulogist before the service and make sure to work through questions of timing, propriety, and purpose. With respect to timing, encourage the eulogist to be no longer than five minutes. It's a random number, but you get the point: brevity is next to spirituality. There will be more stories than what can be included. The eulogist will need to be selective. Selectivity is controlled not only by timing but also by propriety. I encourage people to ask themselves whether a church is the best setting for any story. If the eulogist feels the need to preface a story with an apology, then that story is best not told in that setting but left for the reception (if it needs to be told at all). And finally, purpose. The eulogy is a family's way of setting their grief and all its attendant emotions before God and God's people. It is a way of communicating to them that God and his church are present with them even here. Not every memory contributes to that purpose, and if it doesn't, it ought not to be shared there.

Next, Scripture readings. A churched family will likely have Scripture chosen before they meet with you. But this eventuality is rarer all the time. Many will have some inkling of something from the Bible that they would like read. "You know, Pastor, the one about the sheep," was all the direction I was given for a graveside service during the COVID-19 pandemic. And so I centered my homily on John 10 and Psalm 23. Some will have no idea at all and say, "We trust you to pick something." The temptation in this instance is to proceed with the cookie-cutter Scripture and sermon based on a familiar passage—Psalm 121 or Ecclesiastes 3 or John 14. In those cases, you will need to be more directive when you help your family plan, but resist the temptation to let them off the hook. This is an opportunity to do a little Bible study. Bring a list of Scriptures for them to read through and reflect on. It need not be a long one, and in-depth study is, of course, not possible. But here is an opportunity for the pastor to apply the proclaimed word in a personal, private setting—one in which the people may well be more open to hearing such application than at any other time. One way to make the most of this opportunity is to bring with you a short list of potential Scripture passages from across the canon, including the Old Testament, Gospels, and Epistles. Offering options will empower your family to make a choice and free them from being overwhelmed by the unfamiliar.

Finally, hymns. It has become a truism since the Arian crisis of the fourth century that Christians learn what they sing, and it is also true that corporate singing, of any sort, is a casualty of late modernity. Even churches where congregational singing and choirs have been slower to die sometimes seem either resigned to that end or, worse, eager to embrace hymnic euthanasia for the sake of the mythical seeker or young family. That casts hymn selection in a peculiarly difficult light.

And yet hymns are an important part of liturgy, helping to make the performance a truly corporate one. Hymns make the singing. The challenge here is selection. Many songs that people want at their funeral don't really belong there. Some—Bette Midler's "From a Distance," for example—are simply wrong and, despite being catchy, don't belong in a Christian service of worship. Other songs play more on people's sentimentality than anything else—Vince Gill's "Go Rest High on that Mountain" comes to mind. When songs like these are raised, appealing to the reception is always a good idea, not least because the songwriters of most of them never dreamed that they would be sung as part of a worship service. Bring a hymnbook to your meeting so you can help the family select based on content rather than mood or sentimentality. (And as with Scriptures, make some basic selections beforehand so they're not overwhelmed with options.)

Because of their focus on the coming of Christ, Advent hymns are particularly adaptable to a funeral setting. Of course, "O Come Emmanuel" is too associated with Christmas to be of much use, but "Lo! He Comes with Clouds Descending" is on my short list that I have provided families. Hymns that speak of resting in Christ, hope in his resurrection, and vindication in the coming judgment are all suitable. Anglicans and Methodists are especially blessed to have Charles Wesley's hymns at their disposal. To my mind, Wesley, perhaps uniquely, has blended the theological with rich pastoral application. I have specifically requested "Rejoice, the Lord Is King!" with its promise of a hopeful encounter with the Judge-Redeemer to be sung at my funeral. Recently a dear friend and mentor in ministry celebrated the seventieth anniversary of his ordination. As part of his testimony to mark the occasion, he quoted the final stanza of Charles Wesley's hymn, "Jesus! The Name High over All."

> Happy, if with my latest breath
> I may but gasp His name:
> Preach Him to all, and cry in death,
> Behold, behold the Lamb![58]

Not everyone can sing those words or have them sung. They are too weighty. But my friend, whose ministry and life are now well past twilight, can. And I expect they will be sung with enthusiasm when we commend his mortal remains to the ground and his spirit to God who gave it. I have been blessed to have been formed in singing congregations, both Anglican and the larger Methodist family, with rich, overlapping but not identical hymnic traditions. I recognize that my experience is increasingly marginal. I cannot recommend newer hymns to younger colleagues in ministry. And yet, I cannot be silent about newer hymns. For me, the benchmark of a Christ- and gospel-centered hymn of hope is Keith Getty's and Stuart Townend's "In Christ Alone." Written in 2001, it may not be a new hymn anymore, but for those of us more at home in the 1700s and earlier, 2001 is but yesterday. Any newer song that approaches its depth of content and simple statement will work.

Scripting the Service

When it comes time to script the service, simplicity and unoriginality are the watchwords. Remember the power of words, especially familiar ones. Like a poorly chosen eulogy story, fresh or unfamiliar rhetorical flourishes will draw the attention away from God and toward the speaker and their idiosyncrasies. At the outset of this book, I spoke of a family for whom those words may as well have been a magical incantation. From the expression on their faces, it was obvious they had no idea what was going on. I need now to be clear: that was a failure not on their part for leaving

the church their family had attended for generations. Nor was it the fault of the culture of late
modernity that had so successfully dechurched
them. It was my fault for failing to take my pastoral tasks as catechist and liturgist as seriously
as I should have. I should have spent more time
with them, worked through the actual service with
them, and been more directive at key points than
I was. The unchurched and dechurched families
you will face might not be familiar with the funeral
service. That does not mean you ought to alter it
significantly to suit them; rather, it's a call to be
more explanatory beforehand. Once people have
an idea of what the words will do, the words will,
in fact, do their work.

Thus, the strongest piece of advice I can offer
here is this: if your denomination or ecclesial community or congregation has a funeral manual, a
funeral liturgy, or a prayer book of some sort, use
it! Bring it to the meeting with your family; work
through it with them; explain each major movement beforehand so they will have a sense of what's
going on. Don't be original. You and I cannot, over
the space of a few days, assemble a service that will

accomplish what one that has been painstakingly developed over centuries can.

Nevertheless, there will be occasions when conducting this service in its entirety is not possible, and you will have to adapt, whether by piecing together various parts or by conducting your own. Services in a funeral home chapel will differ from services at the church. Services for immediate family will differ from those that include the whole church or local community. The most challenging of all will be services at the graveside, which, because of their location and expected brevity, require particular preparatory care.

In such exceptional circumstances, keep the purpose and tasks from the previous chapter at the forefront of your plans. At a funeral, as at every Christian worship service, the purpose is to glorify God through the proclamation of and response to the gospel. Specifically, a funeral will commit the deceased to God's care, comfort the bereaved with God's love, and call the living to repentance in the hope of God's gracious judgment. The following outline is simple and easily adapted to several settings; I use it regularly in funeral homes and at the graveside.

The Gathering

The first movement of the service, as indeed any worship service, is to gather the community. The funeral is unique insofar as one of those gathered is not in fact present. The gathering ought to highlight the liminal nature unique to the funeral. We have gathered at the community's existential edge to send a loved one across the threshold into eternity, the community of the dead, the church triumphant. For this reason, we acknowledge and announce God as Lord of both communities at the outset. This can be done in several ways. A traditional funeral will process with clergy, the deceased's remains, and the family, but a procession is not necessary. Well-chosen introductory Scripture sentences (the Anglican [Canadian] *Book of Alternative Services* includes John 11:25–26, John 14:1–3, and Romans 8:38–39) or a hymn or congregational song will accomplish the task.

A psalm to give voice to the place where the community is gathered might then follow. Families often choose Psalm 23 regardless of their level of Christian commitment, and it fits easily here. There are, of course, many psalms that speak of God's presence in times of distress and death, that call out to God for deliverance and so on. This psalm will allow all present to give voice to their grief and bring that grief inside the language of the church. Inviting the community to read the psalm aloud together or responsively with you may help.

If there will be a eulogy, it should be placed here, before the readings and sermon, where it has less chance to decenter or even derail the funeral. More importantly, it serves to remind the community of the deceased's place in the community and their absence from that community, preparing it to mark a significant departure. The eulogy is not a retirement roast, and while humor is often an important element in a good eulogy, the liturgical purpose needs to be kept in mind.

The gathering concludes with a prayer of invocation and a hymn or song. Here, the community's loss ought to be acknowledged, God's comfort sought, and the hope of resurrection mentioned. This moment will serve as a transition to the hearing of the Word of God.

The Word

Though the service has already been rightly saturated with Scripture, this does not replace the Word read as an act of divine address. In this context, the Scriptures comprise God's speech to us in this moment and ought to be read in such a way. If a family member or friend has been asked to read one of the lessons, invite them to practice. The reading does not need to be dramatic or precious or even perfect. But it ought to sound like it has been lovingly prepared and delivered so as not to distract listeners from its content. There may be two or even three lessons prepared (decided in advance with the family), but I recommend that the last be a reading from a Gospel. The community and the family needs to know that Jesus himself is present by his Spirit, speaking and ministering—that he has gathered with us at a grave. And so, John 10 (the Good Shepherd), John 11 (the death of Lazarus), or John 14 (Jesus as the Way), may well be read here.

Following the reading of Scripture, it must be proclaimed. The pastoral task here is the same as it is for every homily or sermon: to open up the text to the gathered community, showing how it is brought within the scriptural narrative such that the story describes their experience and plots the way forward. While you may well refer to the deceased, especially if you knew them, this is not a second eulogy. The funeral homily or sermon is an address to the living, alerting them to God's presence in their loss and grief, comforting them, strengthening them, and calling them to repentance and faith, all with the good news of the gospel.

The Response

After hearing the Word, the community then responds. More liturgically-oriented congregations will begin their response with an affirmation of faith, usually the Apostles' Creed. If this is not part of your tradition, you can move to the responsory prayer. Here is another opportunity for community or family participation. Again, however, the caution associated with eulogies needs to be kept in mind: keep the focus on God. A prepared prayer (rather than extempore or homemade) is usually best. Ensure the whoever is praying has the prayer in advance in order to practice it. Many funeral liturgies will conclude the responsory prayer with a communal recitation of the Lord's Prayer; this is appropriate. However, consider the use of language. Most of your people, if they have committed the prayer to memory, will remember the old language ("art in heaven," "thy name," "trespasses," etc.), so stick with it. If the need for a contemporary language version is clear (for example, the community gathered is almost entirely unchurched), include it in a service leaflet.

Following the responsory prayer, it is time for the deceased to leave the community for the final time. Liturgically, this is accomplished through a prayer of commendation that may resemble this one:

> Into your hands, O merciful Saviour,
> we commend your servant, [Name].
> Acknowledge, we pray, a sheep of your own
>   fold,
> a lamb of your own flock,
> a sinner of our own redeeming.
> Receive him/her into the arms of your
>   mercy,
> Into the blessed rest of everlasting peace,
> And into the glorious company of the saints
>   in light.[59]

Notice that the focus remains on God and God's mercy, reminding all assembled that though lost to us, the deceased is not lost to God. Whatever joys will be experienced in God's presence, they rest on God's redeeming grace and not the attainment of a particular level of piety or morality in this life. This prayer is indeed a prayer to God, but pastorally, the task is toward the family, readying them to say their final goodbye.

The Committal

That final goodbye is the committal of the remains to their final resting place. Now, unfortunately, as a result of the rapid growth of alternative means of disposal, the commital is increasingly an afterthought. Unlike ashes, a body cannot be stored in a closet; regardless of the weather, something has to be done with it. In colder climates, the committal may be postponed because a grave cannot be dug due to frost. But this is an exceptional circumstance, an extended interruption in the one act of worship. Encourage your family to have the committal, if possible, immediately following the funeral. It is a bodily act of leaving their loved one in their new community that will reinforce all that has already happened and help with the grieving process. Liturgically, it is the natural end. We have brought the deceased to where they need to be, where they could not have gotten on their own, and now we must return to the community of the living, to the church militant, there to continue in God's grace and mercy until the next time.

Again, reassembling at the cemetery or colum-
barium should be clothed in the words of holy
Scripture. God's Word, and therefore, God himself,
is present even here. The words that are spoken
should focus the assembled on the hope of the
resurrection. There are any number of prayers of
committal available to you. I consistently use the
one from my own training in the Anglican Church
and offer it here:

> In sure and certain hope of the resurrection
> to eternal life
> through our Lord Jesus Christ,
> we commend to almighty God our brother/
> sister [Name],
> and we commit his/her body to the ground;
> earth to earth, ashes to ashes, dust to dust.
> The Lord bless him/her and keep him/her,
> the Lord make his face to shine upon him/
> her and be gracious to him/her,
> the Lord lift up his countenance upon him/
> her
> and give him/her peace. Amen.[60]

During the prayer of committal, there is often a
symbolic casting of earth into the grave. It need not

be symbolic. At my wife's grandfather's funeral, we followed a long family tradition of literally passing a shovel among the men in the family—Artie's sons and sons-in-law, followed by his grandsons and his granddaughters' spouses. We left the grave only when it was full. Our duties to God, to Artie, and to each other were over, and there was no clearer way to say so. This is an exceptional circumstance, but it helps underscore the importance of the committal as a whole and the symbolic casting of earth in particular. If the family wishes to do this, do not discourage it!

Prayers for the family as they continue to mourn may follow here, and then finally, a benediction that deliberately sends the assembled away from the community of the dead and back to the community of the living, there to resume the process of life before the face of God, brings the funeral to a close.

PRACTICE, PRACTICE, PRACTICE

Before concluding this chapter, I need to add a note about practice—namely, you need to do it, too. If you are going to ask your eulogist, Scripture readers, or pray-ers to practice beforehand, you need to lead by example. When the funeral begins, you are no longer you. You ought to be immersed in your liturgical role, so familiar and adept with the major moves and language of the service that you will not be overcome with emotion. The family needs space to grieve during the funeral; for their sakes, you cannot. Likewise, being intimately acquainted with what's unfolding will equip you to roll with any surprises. Let me explain.

Joyce was a great friend of my parents and a pillar in the local community. When she died, everyone knew it would be a command performance for all involved at the local Pentecostal church. A large extended family, lots of friends, and community representation all added stress to the pastor's work. And then, fifteen minutes before the funeral was to begin, the pastor was told that the church organist had just died that morning. That catastrophe could well have derailed the whole service. In the changes and chances of this present world, things like these happen. When they do, you need to be so acquainted with your role and your words that your service to your grieving family will take place as smoothly as possible. Well-prepared words will do the work almost regardless of what else is going on around them.

Does this mean that the language of a funeral is magic? Well, it depends. The words are not magic insofar as they raise the dead. Nor are they magic insofar as they provide a shortcut around mourning. They are magic insofar as they are performative. Rightly worked, these words enable us to describe and therefore have eyes to see what is *really* happening. We really are journeying with the dead. They really are leaving us. Having discharged our final duties to them, we really will carry on life without them. Much more importantly, God is really present both to the deceased and to us. The gracious bond—namely, the Lord Jesus made present by the Spirit—that unites us to God and to each other really persists in death. And that really means that the loved one is not lost to God and not lost to us. Thus, the hope of the resurrection is really real! The magic words of the Christian funeral are the closest we can come to the deeper magic from before the dawn of time— words which, when uttered on Easter morning and again at the last day, shall make death work backward.

CHAPTER 8

Evangelist

Preaching is God's work. The preacher just loans
his tongue and hands to God.
—Martin Luther

EMOTIONS RUN HIGH AT FUNERALS, AND FAMILY life can be, well, complicated. I've even seen a police presence in order to keep old feuds outside the chapel. But I've only ever been angry at a funeral once. It was a chapel service, and I was assisting the funeral director. The family's minister arrived only about two minutes before we were to begin. Once we had seated the family, the funeral began. The service proceeded normally until the sermon. I don't have a great memory, but I can quote the sermon in its entirety. Here it is. "When I was driving here this morning, I saw a sign that read

'Live, Laugh, Love.' That's good advice, especially on days like today. Amen." As I write this memory, I still feel a little fire that could be easily stoked. I could not and cannot believe that a preacher of the gospel could stand literally between the living and the dead and say ... that.

My reaction was strong—perhaps disproportionately so—because in my own understanding of the ministry of Word and sacrament, the Word looms large. It is the gospel promise in the Word that is to be proclaimed audibly in the sermon and visibly in water, bread, and wine. When that Word is reduced to—or worse, substituted for— two banal sentences cribbed from a greeting card, the Word has not failed, but the preacher certainly has. Rather than being the Word's ambassador, welcoming the Word into the lives of the people to whom he speaks, the preacher has helped bar the door against it. There's no underestimating the weight of responsibility here. The preacher stands between the living and the dead.

Recall the parable of the rich man and Lazarus from chapter 4. Finding himself in hell, the rich man asks for Lazarus to be sent back to the world of the living to warn the rich man's brothers. Abraham's reply is stark: "They have Moses and the prophets." They have, in other words, God's Word. It is no less true today. Until the last day, the doorway to eternity admits in only one direction. Until the last day, we have God's Word promising, warning, and comforting. You are tasked with opening that Word to a family that needs to hear it and are as close to Lazarus-come-back as they'll get. Greeting card sentiments aren't good enough.

The great nineteenth-century Baptist preacher Charles Spurgeon regularly reminded himself and his hearers that while the Reformer Martin Luther feared no human authority, he never ascended into the Wittenberg pulpit without his knees knocking lest he fail to be faithful to God and his Word.[61] Sometimes my knees have knocked like Luther's (or Spurgeon's, for that matter), though not as often as I should like. Nevertheless, it remains my goal always to remember where I am, whose I am, and to whom I speak, and never let it become routine.

Hopefully, you agree that the funeral sermon, as God's Word proclaimed, is of central importance. But just what is that funeral sermon to do? It is to do no less and no other than the service itself: to glorify God by committing the deceased to God's care, comforting the bereaved with the promise of the gospel, and calling the living to repentance and faith. That's the task. Always. You are not there to provide therapy or counsel—which ought to come both before and, hopefully, after. Nor are you there to lighten the mood with humorous memories or cliched illustrations. You are there to declare the good news that the Judge is the Redeemer who, by his life, has reconciled us to God; that he alone will write the last word over their loved one's life; and that these announcements are true not simply in general, nor only for the deceased, but *for them*. The funeral sermon is to announce the good news, the evangel. And that makes you, standing as you are between the dead and the living, not just a preacher. You are an evangelist.

Preparation

A good funeral sermon, like every sermon, involves preparation, practice, and good delivery. And yet, any pastor will tell you that a funeral sermon is different both from the typical Sunday morning homily and from those sermons that mark other special occasions. A confluence of three factors marks a funeral sermon as distinct. Perhaps the most significant is timing. Even in these days of sometimes indefinite postponement between death and burial, funeral sermons still have to be put together quickly. The temptation here will be to over-rely on the work of others. Google "funeral sermons," and you will find many free and fee-based services that are happy to provide customers with notes or even a full manuscript that is easily adapted. There is certainly nothing wrong with consulting such websites or manuals for these sorts of aids; there *is* something wrong when they become an alternative to your own preparation. Families have come to you and want to hear from God through you. There is no easy shortcut.

This is not to say that every sermon will be fresh from the keyboard. A friend of mine, a preacher for many decades, often quips that if a sermon was worth preaching only once, it wasn't worth preaching the first time. A good funeral sermon is one that lends itself to adaptation to another family's grief—not least because there are a limited number of Scripture texts to which you will frequently return for reflection, usually at the family's request. It is not a shortcut, or at least not a harmful one, to have work reappear often. There are only so many sermons in, for instance, Psalm 23 or John 14:1–2. My typical small-town, interrelated funeral congregation brings the same people back regularly, and more than once I have received the comment, "I've heard that sermon before." However, it's intended, I always hear in that remark that the person was, in fact, listening. That's always good. Given the perennial challenge of timing, reusing material is wise. Keep notes and manuscripts ready for repurposing and reuse.

At the same time, however, this sermon ought to be uniquely prepared for the close friends and family members who will hear it. For their sakes, don't offer a generic meditation. Adapt, repurpose, and reuse, certainly—but do not repeat. Ever. Keep the people you've met with, who shared their stories and helped you pick hymns and Scriptures, in mind as you adapt, rework, and renew your material. Use their names, stories, and memories to help them see how the life of their loved one finds its place in the narration of the gospel—the good news of the Word-made-flesh who conquered death, and whose life has been poured out in our hearts by the Holy Spirit.

The consideration of the audience to which I've just gestured is the funeral sermon's second difference. Most likely, you will have a different audience than your usual congregation. It will vary in terms of age, stage of life, and level of discipleship or faith commitment. More importantly, unlike at most weddings, people will actually be listening. You are announcing the gospel—the good news of a crucified and risen Savior who is Lord of life and death, and you are announcing it to *this* group of people and not another. What of the good news do they most need to hear? The specifics will change with each situation.

Nevertheless, it's wise to remember to keep it simple in two ways. My temptation in every sermon is to over-complicate things, and I consciously have to work toward simple while avoiding simplistic. Simple also has to do with application. Although the sermon is mostly for the family present, it is the Word proclaimed to the whole assembled community. That means intricacy in application ought not to be indulged. There is a time for that important work. I'll say more about that in the next chapter.

The need for simplicity flows into the third factor: urgency. A funeral sermon is an urgent sermon. Standing between the living and the dead, you don't have time for the trite, the trivial, or the banal. The thin place between the communities of the living and the dead is a serious place to be and needs to be taken as such. This is not to say a funeral sermon ought to be without humor. I am from a laughing family. Between 2016 and 2019, we buried a beloved uncle, aunt, and my father. All three church funerals were full of laughter, even as we mourned our great loss. We had to speak of my Uncle Hugh's endless tricks and funny stories, my Aunt Norma's intensity, and my dad's home-spun wisdom. As a family, we took solace in that laughter because it meant they were missed by many people. The laughter for us meant that we weren't alone in our grief. But there was no escaping the gravity of what was taking place. Those funerals were moments of reckoning in which all present were invited to consider their own mortality, the possibility of transcendence, and the realities of judgment and hope in Christ. No one left that church having not heard, in simple terms, the gospel promise, which brought both comfort and call.

Keeping the challenges that come with timing, audience, and urgency in mind, a funeral sermon is prepared and delivered like any other. The preacher's task is twofold: to open the text and then to invite people into it. Open the text, first of all, to yourself through the disciplines of good exegesis. Investigate your text's individual words and grammatical structure as well as the literary, historical, and canonical contexts. Look at the history of its interpretation. A funeral sermon's needed simplicity is not permission to avoid the hard work of preparation: original languages if possible, biblical encyclopedias and dictionaries, good commentaries, and multiple English translations. Make the text transparent to yourself. Only then can you work toward making it transparent to the people who will gather. Having opened the text to yourself, you now open it to others. You move, in other words, from what the text *says* to what it *says to your hearers on this specific occasion.*

That is the move from exegesis to exposition. A funeral sermon ought to be an expository sermon, not in the sense that it is a verse-by-verse commentary on the text, but that it opens the text to the congregation so they can discern its meaning for their time and situation. If, for example, the family has chosen Psalm 23, you will no doubt reflect on what the text means when it speaks of comfort in the valley of the shadow of death, of feasting, healing, and abundance—all in the presence of enemies, and all a result of the constant presence of the Shepherd. You may well highlight the subtle shift from the third person in the opening scene of upland meadows to the second person in the darkest valley. But of course you would not stop there. You would move to a reflection on the abiding presence of the Shepherd for your hearers and the means to discern it.

Having opened the text, a good funeral sermon will invite hearers to live within it. I deliberately do not say "apply" it. That is to move in precisely the wrong direction. It has seemed to me for some time that "applying" the text is bringing the Word of God to a basically intact life, and inviting people to pick and choose what fits and what does not: "four ways to cope with grief," being the funerary equivalent to "five tips for a happy marriage." Death, however, shatters the intact life such that there may well be nothing to receive the application. The Lutheran theologian George Lindbeck often spoke of "the text absorbing the world."[62] That should be the goal of every sermon, but especially so at a funeral. When preachers invite their hearers into the text, they give people the words they need to express and understand what has happened: they really are in the valley of the shadow of death, and really do need a Good Shepherd to protect, to comfort, to feed, and to heal. And the good news, however hard it may be to see at the moment, is that he *is there.* That's the truth that sets even the grieving free.

The invitation takes place in three movements. In the first, place the life of the deceased inside the text. How does that life, now gone from us, continue to be held within the Word and hands of God? Was that life itself a book on whose pages God's Word was written? How? Where? Personal stories of the deceased are essential to a good funeral sermon. But the stories serve the Word, not the other way around. Second, place the lives of the living in the text. How does the text narrate or place or illumine where they are now? How does it give an account of their suffering over the previous days or months? How might it lay out a map of the future as they navigate the long process of grieving? How does it alert them to Christ's presence in the midst not simply of suffering, but, much more acutely, of *their* suffering? Finally, point to Christ as the source of hope in the midst of grief and the way to eternal life. A funeral may not be the occasion to quote Pope St. John Paul II's ringing declaration, "Be not afraid! Open wide the doors to Christ!" But it is the time to capture the essence of that simple gospel invitation and present it to people who, whether they recognize it or not, need to hear it.

Delivery

The average attention span is already short, and under the stress that comes with all funerals, it's even shorter. In terms of delivery, then, the funeral sermon ought first of all to be brief—certainly not as brief as the sermon I mentioned at this chapter's outset, but also no longer than seven to ten minutes (or about twice the length of a good eulogy). If the service has been carefully prepared beforehand—whether it is a sanctioned liturgy well performed or a free church format—the congregation will have been soaked in Scripture long before the sermon. And by the illuminating Spirit, the Word will do its work. At a funeral, no less than at any Sunday sermon, the preacher is a servant of the Word, bringing forth treasures new and old. The focus ought to be on the treasures. While stories that place the deceased and the family inside the Word are important, don't clutter your sermon with them. The eulogy hopefully will have taken care of some of that, and the reception afterward (see the next chapter) will help, too. Serve the

Word and let the Word work. And at a funeral, such service is necessarily minimalist.

Second, be simple. Preparation needs to involve good exegesis. The content ought to be expository, but exegesis and exposition are not the product itself. One of the best funeral sermons I've heard took as its text John 1:6: "There was a man sent from God, whose name was John." Prepared for the family of a fellow minister, this sermon skillfully brought both John (the deceased) and his family into the text, placing him and them in the place of John the Baptist as a servant of the Word-made-flesh. I can only imagine the temptation here to leave thoughtful exegesis and good exposition behind for the sake of the obvious and immediate emotional appeal. But that is not what the preacher did. Instead, the text became a window through which we could see John the minister's life as a servant of the Word, a servant for whom John the Baptist was the exemplar. The sermon ended with an invitation for all of us to be similar servants in our various vocations. This sermon was not elaborate or complicated. Its simplicity made its content of lasting comfort to all who attended.

Finally, be direct. John Stott titled his classic book on preaching *Between Two Worlds*; he meant the world of the Bible and the world of today. More sharply drawn, however, is the distinction between the worlds of the living and the dead. The preacher stands between these two communities every Sunday, though, from the content of many sermons, it might be difficult to tell. The intersection of the two is especially clear at the funeral because it is so literal. Still, do not confuse direct with harsh. Of course, we need to speak in a way that will not snuff out a smoldering wick or break a bent reed[63] among the mourners. But we are wise not to confuse that important pastoral counsel with florid or schmaltzy sermons that tickle the ears while avoiding the questions everyone in the room is asking—questions of destiny, transcendence, presence, judgment, and hope.

Once, when Henry VIII arrived at Canterbury Cathedral, apparently unannounced, Archbishop Hugh Latimer was said to have begun his sermon with these words: "Latimer, Latimer, thou art going to speak before the high and mighty King, Henry VIII, who is able, if he think fit, to take thy life away. Be careful what thou sayest. But Latimer, Latimer, remember also thou art about to speak before the King of kings and Lord of lords. Take heed that thou dost not displease Him."[64] At a funeral, preachers stand in the presence of death and need, as a result, to show tremendous care in their delivery. But even more than that, they stand in the presence of the Life that conquers death, charged with making their words fit vehicles for his Word. That is the reason why a good preacher's knees knock both at the desk and in the pulpit.

HARD CASES

"Hard cases make bad law." This legal maxim, invoked in various forms since at least 1837, means that a legal decision in a complicated case ought not to be used as a precedent to cover a much broader range of situations. However true the adage may be for the courtroom or the legislature, it is undoubtedly true with funeral sermons. Tragic deaths—the hard cases that every preacher must at some point address—are invariably unique. And while what I've written above will impinge upon the preacher's important work even here, it will do so only in the most general of ways. Every minister who has a decade or so of experience has a file of these cases: a child, an adolescent, a suicide, an accident. And every minister will tell you that each situation is different; that what needs to be said in the light of God's Word at one child's graveside absolutely cannot be said at another's. In a previous chapter, I mentioned the importance of a ministry mentor who can bring their direct experience into conversation with yours—not to provide you with the right words to say, but to offer analogous situations to help you work out what you *need* to say. I do so again here. A manual like this one, while I hope it is helpful, simply cannot duplicate these sorts of conversations.

In my own experience, which is thin compared to that of many others, I am made especially aware of my priestly identity. Set aside debates about ordination; the word "priestly" is valid whether you're a Baptist or an Episcopalian. As a servant, ordained to the ministry of the Word, you stand in the place of Christ in that situation. In your preparation and delivery, you must (like John the Baptist) decrease so that the Lord Jesus can increase. Your words will contain his words. In the hard cases, place the accent on Christ and his words. His saving gospel is balm and salve, even in the most difficult places. His Word will give not mere consolation but comfort—strength. The preacher is his human instrument, his priest. The preacher is a clay vessel at the best of times, but one that contains the priceless treasure of the gospel that, when set out briefly, simply, and directly, will do its work, even if it be at hell's front porch.

CHAPTER 9

Pastor

*We do not do this task of rebuilding our life
narratives alone. In the wilderness of grief,
God provides narrative manna—just enough shape
and meaning to keep us walking—and sends the
Comforter, who knits together the raveled soul
and refuses to leave us orphaned. Sometimes the
bereaved say they are looking for closure, but in the
Christian faith we do not see closure so much as we
pray that all of our lost loves will be gathered into
that great unending story fashioned by God's grace.
—Thomas G. Long*

THE FUNERAL'S OVER, THEN WHAT? FOR MANY
pastors and funeral home chaplains, the answer
is nothing. A few niceties, an exchange of phone
numbers, but that's about it. Once the needed

products and services are provided, the relationship is concluded. This is another advent of modernity in which consumerization, efficiency, hurry, and the denial of our mortality have combined to shortchange people who are grieving. How unlike the Victorians, to whom I alluded in chapter 6. Regarding the funeral not so much as an end as a beginning, their official mourning period could last years and was publicly marked by demeanor and dress.

Today, for many, it is precisely the opposite. The funeral—if that name persists—marks the end of the deceased's journey and of ours with them. All the details surrounding the act itself point to the end: bills to be paid, thank-you cards to be written, estates to be settled. Of course, these all take time, but they are signifiers of an ending rather than a beginning. Even the newer death-vocabulary presses people to move past the event as quickly as possible: "find closure," or "draw a line," or even "get on with life." This topsy-turvy turn flies in the face of human nature. It doesn't square with human experience. Many pastors and funeral directors will acknowledge that when dealing with families, the funeral represents the beginning of a new set of relationships and relational dynamics with the living and even with the dead.

Thus far, we've focused on the funeral itself. But as a friend put it to me, pastors ought to hope for the situation in which, though the funeral's done, they're not. In this final chapter, I'd like to suggest that all that has been written so far marks not the end, but rather the beginning of a profoundly changed pastoral relationship, even if you have pastored the survivors for years already. We have talked about being a catechist, a liturgist, and even an evangelist. Through it all, though, you've already been a shepherd. Now, however, you're embarking with your sheep on a difficult and sometimes perilous journey through the valley of the shadow of death.

The Good Shepherd

There are no more divisive words in Western Christendom than, "This is my body." For Catholic Christians, these words signal the Eucharistic miracle in which the substance of bread and wine is changed into the body and blood of Christ, though the appearance remains unchanged. In this great drama, the priest—an unworthy vessel no doubt—stands in the place of Christ. Indeed, it is Christ himself who says the words of consecration through his servant. The priest at the altar stands in the person of Christ, the head (*in persona Christi capatis*). I don't want to delve into the intricacies of the debates about the nature of ordination that are now, sadly, into their sixth century. I want to deploy the phrase *in persona Christi* to stress just what it is a pastor does for the average parishioner, especially those in times of crisis that include death. The pastor—you—will stand in the place of Christ, mediating his presence, ministering his grace, speaking his Word to people who may well feel as though they've been abandoned by heaven. There's no underestimating the importance of your place and role on this journey. Let's set aside the theological debates surrounding ordination from which this phrase comes. The etymology will do. You're a pastor. A shepherd. You're acting for and even as the Good Shepherd in this specific context.

That's an image that's overwhelmed for many of us by the practical demands of the pastor's day, in which you are part CEO, part counselor, part HR expert, and perhaps groundskeeper (many times, with an entirely other occupation taking up what's left of your time). Pastors need to recover and revive the metaphor of shepherd for their work, especially in North American settings that are increasingly removed from the rural context in which it makes sense. In John 10, Jesus takes the title Good Shepherd to himself, using it to highlight the nature of his ministry as one of faithful presence. A shepherd stays with the sheep. A shepherd tends the sheep. A shepherd protects the sheep. A shepherd heals the sheep. That's what you'll be doing. But not on your own. You'll be doing it with, for, and in the place of Someone Else. You will be there as the visible representation of the Good Shepherd, not as the hired man who flees at the first sign of trouble (John 10:11–13) nor the wicked shepherd who scatters and devours the sheep himself (Ezek 34:1–6). Rather, you will stand in place of the Good Shepherd, who lays down his life for the sheep (John 10:11).

You will stand in the place of Christ the head, speaking his word, acting in his name, allowing him to speak and act through you. This is neither to discomfit you nor to exalt your office. It is, rather, to highlight how many people for whom you care will regard you. Life crises, especially death, may even in the most committed Christian sever felt ties with the divine. They will need to be shown—far more than merely told—that even in the valley of the shadow of death, Christ has not abandoned them; that he is, to recall Luther's *theology of the cross*, with them even to the point of being with them on the cross of their trial. They need to know that Christ is there. They will know because you are there. There in the symbols of your office—Bible, collar, stole, and sacrament. Because a good shepherd has committed to not leaving them until they dwell in the Lord's house forever, they will know that the Good Shepherd continues with them even if he seems withdrawn.

I Will Fear No Evil

"Though I walk through the valley of the shadow of death, I will fear no evil for you are with me" (Ps 23:4). The psalmist's "you," of course, is the LORD, who has provided for him in green pastures, by still waters and along the paths of righteousness (vv. 1–3). The psalmist straightforwardly acknowledges the ultimate source of that provision but signals that here in those sun-turned uplands, the Lord himself is distant. Described only in the third person, "he," God's provision and leadership is acknowledged when all is well, but he's neither near nor needed. At the threshold of the valley, however, the person changes from third to second, from "he" to "you." The ministry of the Shepherd is a ministry of presence, especially when his presence may feel remote, even absent. Most of us who are grieving will express (even if only to ourselves) sentiments similar to those of C. S. Lewis, who, upon the death of his wife, Joy, wrote this:

> When you are happy, so happy you have no sense of needing Him, so happy that you are tempted to feel His claims upon you as an interruption, if you remember yourself and turn to Him with gratitude and praise, you will be—or so it feels—welcomed with open arms. But go to Him when your need is desperate, when all other help is vain, and what do you find? A door slammed in your face, and a sound of bolting and double bolting on the inside. After that, silence.[65]

You, a shepherd acting in the place of *the* Shepherd, will by your mere presence be a reminder of the reality of Christ's presence in the midst of a profound absence.

And not only a reminder, but also a vehicle. It is a recurring theme in the ministry of Martin Luther that he did nothing while the Word did everything.

Broadly stated, to be sure, but it highlights an important dynamic at work here. The idea is not so much that as a pastor, you are entirely passive, an unconscious agent if you will. It is, rather, that as you go about your work, you are a vehicle for the Word who alone can do the work that needs doing. The psalmist describes God's Word as a lamp and light that guides in the darkness. You are not the Word; you are in cooperation with the Spirit, the breath on which it is carried. You are not the light. You may well be the wick. Without for a moment underestimating or downplaying the importance of training in ministry, the focus is not on your expertise, or your wisdom. You hone those skills and practice those words so that they can be fit vehicles for the one illuminating and healing Word.

As a reminder of the reality of Christ in the midst of death, your presence will be the sacramental means through which Christ provides the antidote to the existential fear that comes with the awful awareness of death's shadow. I was reminded of this powerfully by the movie *Calvary*, in which Father James (Brendan Gleeson) goes about the mundane business of being a priestly presence, the larger-than-life representative of a morally diminished institution. In a dying community, to the lives of ordinary parishioners, Father James serves the sacrament, visits the sick, and gently calls his people to repentance, all the while knowing that one of these very people will kill him in one week's time. Father James ministers in the shadow of death—the death of the Catholic Church in Ireland, the death of a traffic victim, the death of his dog, the little deaths exemplified in the sins of the people for whom he cares, and most especially his own impending death. The fear he experiences—as real as that experienced in Gethsemane—is not one that paralyzes or provokes a flight from danger, though he is given both opportunity and episcopal permission. Father James remains faithful even to his own Good Friday and his own Calvary. Obviously, the film makes its point using extreme images. I doubt that any of us will conduct our ministry under such trial. Still, it's this sort of presence to the very end, embodied in the work of Father James, that will calm the fears of the anxious souls to which you minister. And it is just this sort of presence that is choked out by many of the responsibilities that come with being a "successful" pastor.

The Rod and the Staff

Your abiding presence will assuage fear; it will also, in so doing, provide protection. The psalmist speaks of the shepherd's tools—the rod and the staff—providing comfort. They are tools that keep enemies at bay and sheep in line, giving the sheep courage to continue through the valley. While it might be grimly soothing to long for a rod to rap a wolf on the head or a staff to yank a lamb back from the brink, the tools of your trade are different. You are a minister of Word and sacrament. Bible, water, bread, and wine: those are your tools. Christ's life therein alone can keep the enemies at bay and the sheep from falling. Yours is indeed a ministry of presence, but not because you're you. It is a ministry of the presence of he who comes with you, in, with, and under your tools. He will keep the enemies at bay. He will keep them from harming those for whom you care and, indeed, from harming you.

Here we are wise to recapture the biblical image of death as an enemy, again an increasingly countercultural notion. As an on-call palliative care chaplain for a local hospice, I have heard a great deal about how death is a natural part of life, that it is not to be feared, but accepted with as much equanimity as possible. As a palliative care advocate, I affirm the need of people to die, if not in their own homes, in as much of a home-like atmosphere as possible, surrounded by people who care for and can comfort them. Still, I can't bring myself to affirm the language in which such comfort is often couched. I have heard others describe their loved ones' deaths as something profoundly unnatural and even hostile. I experienced my father's death as indeed a holy moment but one that gave way to something horrid as we waited for the funeral director to come and take his body away. It was as though death had entered his room. Death is an enemy, *the* enemy—the great breaker of all the bonds that make us, us. From him and his minions, we need protection.

"Did we in our own strength confide, the battle would be losing!"[66] I have turned to this hymn before in this book, but not without reason. How right Martin Luther's great hymn is. We cannot stand against death, in our own strength, on his own turf, there in the valley. But we are not alone, as Luther goes on to remind us. The right man of God's own choosing *is* on our side. He has determined never to leave nor forsake his sheep. And he will win (indeed, has won!) the battle against sin, death, and the devil. The old gospel song is surely right to say that "you've got to walk that lonesome road … by yourself." However much we might be surrounded by those we love, at the end, it will only be you, me, alone dying. But the song is right to insist that even on death's lonesome road, "I've got to hold my Savior's hand." Jesus—God and man in the unity of his person—has descended to the dead. And he will descend again with his sheep: he will accompany them even there, and at the moment of their deaths, they will surrender not to an implacable enemy but to his gracious and victorious presence. He is with your sheep because he is with you, because you carry the means by which he comes to them, protects and keeps them, and reminds both the sheep and the enemy who seeks their souls that death is defeated—that death cannot finally undo us.

Feasting in the Face of the Enemy

Enlivened by the presence of Christ, you will even prepare a feast in the presence of those very enemies, ensuring your sheep can dine while the enemies can only watch from a distance. I never paid attention to that image until I read an editorial by a rabbi following the September 11 terrorist attacks.

Drawing on Psalm 23, he dwelled especially on the presence of enemies. He spoke not so much of the sheep being comforted and protected—which is where my mind always went first—as of the frustration of the enemies. Compelled to watch by the armed-and-ready Shepherd, they could do nothing but gnash their teeth in frustration as the Shepherd's beloved ones ate and drank and made merry in their presence. It is a sign of God's victory and a surety of his coming kingdom that de-fanged death is made to watch us when we feast in his face. Fearsome, iron-scaled, fire-breathing Leviathan is baited and made God's pet (Job 41). God's life-giving Word enables us, like Samson, to pull honey from a carcass and eat (Judg 14:9). Feasting in the face of death is God's promise, our defiance, and death's defeat, all wrapped up in an egg salad sandwich.

An egg salad sandwich may seem a trivial thing, but it's not. A reception—egg salad sandwiches and all—following the funeral is concrete evidence of this profound spiritual reality. In my Northern Irish heritage, the reception is often a joyous event. The reality of the family's grief is neither denied nor ignored but set in the broader contexts of church and family support. The reception is the first opportunity to display bonds of affection in the larger community, a reminder that God's abiding presence will continue in and through God's abiding people. Singer-songwriter Bob Bennet captures the right and proper sense of funerary feasting in his song *The Place I Am Bound*, and especially in these words:

> I wish I could be there to lighten the mood
> With friends and family and mountains of
>   food
> And stories and memories and tales all
>   around
> But it's late and I must travel to the place I
>   am bound.[67]

There is no denial of loss and absence, but these are recontextualized in the space of feasting—and indeed, in the presence of Life, for whom death, while an enemy, is defeated. An interruption in a longer story in which each chapter is better than the last.

HEALING

And this serves as a reminder that your pastoral presence is a healing one. You are there to pour oil on bruised heads and bind up battered limbs. The journey back to the land of the living is not easy for any of us. Enemies will snap from the sidelines, and sometimes their teeth will take. Sheep, nearly blind in the darkness of the valley, will through no fault of their own stray from the path that leads to the valley's end. They may need to be pulled away from the brink and might be bruised in the process. Pastors in the name and place of Christ must work to heal the wound and sometimes administer the wounds that heal. The image of anointing with healing oil here implies something that runs against current images of the successful pastor: close contact. The shepherd knows the sheep, and tends, protects, and feeds them. And at the end of the day, he examines them for bruises that need care. There is a level of intimacy the psalmist takes for granted, an intimacy that many urban and suburban pastors simply cannot provide. Insofar as this is true, it suggests to me that we're doing pastoring wrong, not that the psalmist can no longer speak to our day.

So strive especially with those who grieve, to maintain a relationship sufficiently close that you can be an agent of healing. It may be regular weekly visits that slowly become more distanced, or three-month, six-month, and one-year check-ins. If you pastor a large church, you may need to train and commission lay pastors to do this important work. The practicalities will vary across congregational ages, sizes, and places. But the notion of a shepherd who is remote from his sheep, who does not, to use the biblical image, call them by name, is one that is too often accepted as a sacrifice of modern ministry and finds no purchase in the Scriptures. The symbolic imagery evoked by Pope St. John Paul II and now Pope Francis, insisting on being among the people as they travel, exemplifies what I mean here. There is perhaps no more rarified position in global Christianity than the pope of Rome, which is why the imagery of the pontiff being among the people is so powerful. It is a comfort to the laity to be sure; but more so, it is a challenge to priests and bishops that their calling is to be among God's lambs and sheep, feeding them with the Word of the gospel.

Coming Home

The psalmist draws his meditation on the LORD his shepherd to an end with the words, "I shall dwell in the house of the Lord forever" (Ps 23:6 ESV). Your ministry of accompaniment may go through cycles—by still waters, green pastures, and along paths of righteousness for a time, followed by the arduous walk to death's door and back again. When my dad died, a teaching colleague who had buried his wife just two years earlier came from quite a distance for the viewing. When he took my mom's hand, he said, "I didn't bring a card today. I'm going to mail you one in six months. That's when you'll need it." That's what he did; my mom was grateful. He knew as all grieving people do that no matter the amount of suffering that preceded it, the funeral marks a beginning as much as, if not more than, an end. The funeral is the end of the deceased's journey in the land of the living. It is the end of a family's journey with their loved one. But more importantly, for those who mourn it is the beginning of the return journey back into life, back into community, back into the reestablishment and renegotiation of all sorts of relationships. And you as a pastor are a vital part of this reentry.

But going down into the valley and coming out again is not an endless cycle. There is a goal: followed by the Lord's goodness and mercy, you're aiming at the Lord's house, there to remain forever. As a shepherd, you are walking with your sheep in the valley of the shadow of death. But your goal is not simply to get them out and back to "normal," and then to wait until the cycle begins again. Your goal is to lead them to the Lord's house, to heaven. To a creation made fit for the full presence of God. To a full union with Christ and his saints in the church triumphant. To a time and place where every tear shall be wiped away, and death is swallowed up in victory.

Resources

Post-Christendom

> Chaput, Charles. *Strangers in a Strange Land: Living the Catholic Faith in Post-Christian America*. Henry Holt, 2017.

A bracing argument that post-Christendom is culturally different in kind from Christian ways of life and a hopeful call to faithfulness in the midst of such a culture.

> Dreher, Rod. *The Benedict Option: A Strategy for Christians in a Post-Christian Nation*. Sentinel, 2018.

Often criticized as a call to withdraw, this book is more about how to survive as faithful enclaves that have been pushed to the margins by the dominant culture.

➢ Esolen, Anthony. *Out of the Ashes:
   Rebuilding American Culture*. Regnery, 2017.

A call to strengthen mediating institutions—families, churches, local communities—to stand against the corrosions of late modernity.

➢ Milbank, John. *Theology and Social Theory*.
   2nd ed. Wiley-Blackwell, 2006.

John Milbank argues that much of what we take as neutral or scientific social theory rests on an extensive, deliberately anti-Christian history of thought. Christian theology cannot justify itself using this vocabulary. Christianity has its own language, which it must recover, reflect, and reinhabit lest it be absorbed or deconstructed by "secular reason."

➢ Taylor, Charles. *A Secular Age*. Belknap,
   2007.

Charles Taylor offers a history of unbelief in the West: of how agnosticism and atheism became live, intellectual options. For the purposes of this book, his account of the transition of the porous self (that is, one that sees the supernatural and natural worlds as interpenetrating) to the buffered self (that is, one in which they are at first strictly separated, with the supernatural slowly eliminated) helps Christian ministers understand why Christian language (and not just the language of the funeral) can be so foreign to so many people.

ESCHATOLOGY

› Barth, Karl. *The Word of God and the Word of Man*. Peter Smith, 1928.

This early work introduces Barth's claim that the Word of God breaks into the present in a living and active way in the sermon. The Bible is not a text that is sequestered in mythology or history but is the vehicle through which God today unveils both himself and the world when proclaimed in the sermon. Eschatology is an always present reality, for God's Word continues to come to us.

› Bultmann, Rudolf. *History and Eschatology: The Gifford Lectures, 1955*. Edinburgh University, 1957.

This classic work is Bultmann's argument that the coming of Christ or the kingdom is not a future event (whether in millenarian religious terms or secular Marxist ones) but an ever-present, existential reality. Eschatology deals not with the future but with the present. It is timeless.

> Pannenberg, Wolfhart. *Theology and the Kingdom of God.* Westminster John Knox, 1969.

> Moltmann, Jürgen. *Theology of Hope.* SCM, 1967.

These works attempt to reintroduce eschatology as future oriented into Christian theology after Bultmann.

> Lindsey, Hal and Carole C. Carlson. *The Late Great Planet Earth.* Zondervan, 1970.

This book popularized what was, for about a century prior, a fringe view of the last days rooted in the work of J. N. Darby and the Plymouth Brethren known as dispensationalism. A best seller, this book introduced millions of readers to notions of the rapture, tribulation, and millennium to such a degree that these are now taken for granted by many Christians as orthodox eschatology.

➤ LaHaye, Tim and Jerry Walls. *Left Behind*. Tyndale, 1995.

This novel spawned not only a series of books but also a sequel and a series of movies. Taking Lindsey's *Late Great Planet Earth* as its background, it offers a rollicking action-adventure account of those who have been left behind after the rapture of the church. Its money-making success demonstrates just how mainstream dispensational eschatology has become in North American churches.

➤ Ratzinger, Joseph. *Eschatology: Death and Eternal Life*. Ignatius, 1988.

A short handbook on the classic eschatological themes: death, judgment, hell, purgatory, and heaven. It is a clear summary of Christian (Catholic) eschatological teaching that is of tremendous value to all Christians, whether Catholic or not.

➤ Wright, N. T. *Surprised by Hope*. HarperOne, 2008.

This popular book is Wright's attempt to reintroduce the idea of resurrection—both Christ's and ours—into what Christians usually think about heaven and mission, to correct what he understands to be an excessive, unbiblical, and unhelpful other-worldliness.

> Wright, N. T. *History and Eschatology: Jesus and the Promise of Natural Theology.* Baylor, 2019.

This academic work is Wright's attempt to do natural theology as a historian of Jesus and the early church. The eschatological elements—bodily resurrection, parousia, etc.—of early Christian proclamation are set out within the confines of critical historiography.

Death

> Davies, Douglas. *The Theology of Death.* T&T Clark, 2008.

An extensive survey of historical and contemporary ways Christian thought has dealt with death. The third part takes seriously the challenge of thinking Christianly about death in a post-Christian culture.

> Becker, Ernest. *The Denial of Death.* Free
> Press, 1973.

A classic work that argues that civilization from
the bottom up is an elaborate series of attempts
to defend ourselves against the knowledge of our
own mortality. Our "immortality projects," once
provided by religion, are now undermined in the
age of reason. New illusions are necessary, but science cannot provide them.

> Peters, Ted. *Sin: Radical Evil in Soul and
> Society.* Eerdmans, 1994.

Heavily indebted to Paul Tillich, this work seeks
to understand sin not as a list of evil actions but
as the fundamental orientation of human beings
and especially our awareness of our mortality. This
awareness produces anxiety, which could become
the occasion for conversion, but apart from the
work of grace leads to strategies of avoidance (sins)
that only compound the problem.

> Wycliffe College at The University of Toronto. *What Does It Mean to be Human? Ghosts and Machines*. youtu.be/2IYR22ouDP8. Published January 28, 2019.

An interesting debate between artificial intelligence and quantum computing inventor Geordie Rose, cognitive scientist Julien Mussolino, and philosopher of religion Michael Murray on the existence and nature of the soul. Of especial interest is Rose's insistence that while the soul (that is, consciousness) does not exist apart from the brain at present, we will one day be able to upload these neural patterns from dying brains into artificial intelligence matrices. We do not (yet) have souls; we will (soon) build them, thereby obtaining immortality.

Hell

> Hart, David Bentley. *That All Shall Be Saved: Heaven, Hell and Universal Salvation*. Yale University Press, 2019.

David Bentley Hart's four meditations on the moral necessity of universal salvation will only further convince those who already agree with its central thesis, namely, that all will be saved. It is the best articulation of Christian universalism currently available.

> Kvanvig, Jonathan L. *The Problem of Hell*. Oxford, 1993.

Arguing that the retributive understanding of hell (hell as punishment) suffers from intractable problems, Kvanvig develops an alternative yet traditional account that meets the objections made by universalists and annihilationists.

> Lewis, C. S. *The Great Divorce*. Geoffrey Bless, 1946.

Lewis's tour of the outskirts of heaven through the eyes of a group of tourists from hell. Its central idea of hell as an inexorable move away from Reality and toward Nothing and heaven as a move into ever-increasing Reality is especially helpful when thinking about human destiny.

> McClymond, Michael. *The Devil's Redemption: A New Herstory and Interpretation of Christian Universalism.* 2 vols. Baker Academic, 2018.

McClymond's painstakingly thorough history traces the development of various strands of universal salvation—Christian, Jewish, unitarian, etc.—and shows conclusively why Christian universalism has been and will always only be a minority report within global Christianity.

> von Balthasar, Hans Urs. *Dare We Hope That All Men Be Saved? With a Short Discourse on Hell.* 2nd ed. Ignatius Press, 2014.

A classic work in which von Balthasar expresses the hope of universal salvation as opposed to a doctrine of universal salvation. Because it is found in the Scriptures and affirmed in tradition, hell is accepted as a future reality. Nevertheless, we may hope and pray that it will, in the end, be empty.

> Walls, Jerry. *Hell: The Logic of Damnation.* Notre Dame, 1992.

The author argues that some versions of the doctrine of hell are perfectly compatible with both divine and human nature and especially the divine goodness.

HEAVEN

> Burpo, Todd, and Lynn Vincent. *Heaven Is for Real: A Little Boy's Astounding Story of His Trip to Heaven and Back*. Thomas Nelson, 2010.

The title is misleading for at least two reasons: (1) Burpo never actually died, and therefore did not go to heaven. At most it was a vision of heaven suited to the imagination of a young child. (2) More importantly, the book is as much about Todd Burpo's doubts about his son's vision as it is about the details of the vision itself.

> Lewis, C. S. "The Weight of Glory." In *The Weight of Glory and Other Addresses*. Geoffrey Bless, 1949.

Originally preached as a sermon at St. Mary the Virgin, Oxford, this short mediation on heaven's future reality and our present longing is, in my opinion, the best account of heaven in English.

> Malarkey, Alex and Kevin Malarkey. *The Boy Who Came Back from Heaven*. Tyndale, 2010.

A book that will be recalled more for the furor it caused than its actual contents. This near-death experience/trip-to-heaven book and its aftermath shows how dangerous (and lucrative) talking about heaven can be. Read rightly, it reveals more about us than about the afterlife.

> McDannell, Colleen, and Bernhard Lang. *Heaven: A History*. Yale University Press, 1988.

An extensive discussion of how believers have thought about heaven throughout history. The focus on art, literature, and poetry is especially helpful.

> Russell, Jeffrey Burton. *A History of Heaven: The Singing Silence*. Princeton University Press, 1997.

A survey of Christian thought about heaven across the ages, an engagement with the philosophical and theological problems associated with it, and a call to pay more attention to Christian poetry and mystical thought when contemplating eternity.

> Torrance, T. F. *Space, Time and Resurrection.* T&T Clark, 2000.

The resurrection, as traditionally understood, is both true to what Jesus claimed about himself and consonant with current scientific thought. Modern scientific findings, as far as Torrance is concerned, ought not to lead us to compromise the traditional understanding of the bodily resurrection but can reinforce it.

> Updike, John. "Seven Stanzas at Easter." In *Telephone Poles and Other Poems.* Knopf, 1963.

Often read as a triumph of orthodoxy, the poem is far more modest. If (as the poem itself begins) we are to proclaim the resurrection at Easter, then let us proclaim the real thing, lest we lapse into unbelief in our attempts to make it more palatable to modern audiences.

> Wright, N. T. *The Resurrection of the Son of God*. Fortress, 2002.

A mammoth defense of the bodily resurrection of Jesus within the canons of critical historiography. It is an important reminder of the physicality of the resurrection—both of the Easter event and the Christian hope.

> Walls, Jerry. *Heaven: The Logic of Eternal Joy*. Oxford, 2002.

A companion to his philosophical defense of hell, *Heaven* defends a traditional Christian view of eternal bliss and argues that it can address contemporary problems in morality, personal identity, and theodicy. Wall's engagement with near-death experiences equips readers to engage sensitively with "heaven tourism."

Catechist

> Hahn, Scott. *Hope to Die: The Christian Meaning of Death and the Resurrection of the Body*. Emmaus Road: 2020.

Hahn presents a delightfully unoriginal account of death and resurrection. He takes special note of how we treat bodies, both in their dying and afterward.

> Jalland, Pat. *Death in the Victorian Family*. Oxford University, 1996.

An interesting account of the elaborate rituals that came to be associated with dying, death, and mourning in nineteenth-century Britain that contrasts our "make it up as you go" approach today.

> Long, Thomas. *Accompany Them with Singing: The Christian Funeral*. Westminster John Knox, 2009.

The best book on the Christian funeral currently in print. Long contrasts the traditional Christian funeral with contemporary versions and argues that the church ought to reclaim its own language for dying, death, and worship.

> Long, Thomas and Thomas Lynch. *The Good Funeral*. Westminster John Knox, 2013.

In a series of individually authored essays, Long and Lynch describe what a good funeral is and does—or ought to be and accomplish.

➢ Lynch, Thomas. *The Undertaking:*
Life Studies from the Dismal Trade.
Norton, 2009.

Part memoir, part poem, this book introduces the
realities of death—the terrible, sublime, and sometimes absurd—from a small-town funeral director
with a gift for prose.

➢ Menzies, Wade. *The Four Last Things:*
A Catechetical Guide to Death, Judgment,
Heaven, and Hell. EWTN: 2017.

This short introduction to the last things from
a Catholic perspective is a helpful introduction
to both method and content. Easily adapted to
non-Catholic settings.

➢ O'Rourke, Meghan. *The Long Goodbye:*
A Memory of Grief. Riverhead, 2011.

A moving account of a daughter's grief and the very
physical way in which grief is sometimes experienced and addressed.

Liturgist

In this section, I have focused on working with words in general because most denominations and ecclesial communities have their own funerary rites. Few of us are cursed with the freedom to make it up as we go. In the event that you must do so, I recommend borrowing a set denominational liturgy and adapting to your needs. I am convinced that unoriginality is the most important part of funeral liturgy planning.

> Austin, J. L. *How to Do Things with Words.* 2nd ed. Harvard University, 1975.

As the title indicates, this book moves us away from what words mean to what and how words perform. It is not a religious book but does help us think about how the language of worship works (or ought to work).

> Ratzinger, Joseph. *The Spirit of the Liturgy.* Ignatius, 2000.

This is perhaps an odd choice given the audience of this book. But it is a wonderful book on the meaning and significance of Christian worship. Although it is written for a Catholic audience, its deep wisdom communicates across confessional boundaries.

> Soskice, Janet Martin. *Metaphor and Religious Language*. Clarendon, 1987.

Soskice's account of the indispensability and unsubstitutability of metaphors in God-talk has now attained classic status. A powerful reminder that even though much of our liturgical and theological language is metaphorical, recognizing it as such does not grant us permission to change it.

> Williams, Rowan. *The Edge of Words: God and the Habits of Language*. Bloomsbury/ Continuum, 2014.

A series of reflections on how language does and does not work when it comes to talking about God. For our purposes, it helps remind us on the care and attention that is required when constructing a worship service.

EVANGELIST

> Duduit, Michael. "The 25 Most Influential Preaching Books of the Past 25 Years." www.preaching.com/articles/

the-25-most-influential-preaching-
books-of-the-past-25-years/.
Accessed December 22, 2020.

There is no special key to unlock a funeral sermon different from any other kind of sermon. I have included only two works below, not because they are the only ones worth recommending but because there are so many good books on preparing and delivering sermons that I cannot possibly recommend them all. Preaching.com is an invaluable resource worth checking regularly, and for those who wish a beginning bibliography, this article is as good a start as you can get.

➤ Lindbeck, George. *The Nature of Doctrine: Religion and Theology in a Postliberal Age.* Westminster John Knox, 1984.

This book helps preachers rethink what we mean when we talk about applying a text in sermon preparation. Applying ought not to mean bringing tidbits of scriptural wisdom to real life but rather a gospel call out of the false life of the world into the real life of the Bible.

> Stott, John. *Between Two Worlds:*
> *The Challenge of Preaching Today.*
> Eerdmans, 1982.

A classic on contemporary preaching.

PASTOR

> Albom, Mitch. *Tuesdays with Morrie.*
> Doubleday, 1997.

Both a true classic and a best seller, this book is based on weekly conversations between Morrie Schwartz and his former student, Mitch Albom, during the former's final days. A helpful guide to walking with people (both the dying and those who love them) through the last stages of life.

> Gawande, Atul. *Being Mortal: Medicine*
> *and What Matters at the End.* Picador, 2017.

Written by a surgeon, this is an unflinching look at how medicine, in its efforts to preserve life and maintain safety, has made dying more difficult. An essential guide when helping people face hard medical decisions both for those they love and themselves.

➢ Kalinithi, Paul. *When Breath Becomes Air*.
Random House, 2016.

A memoir written by a neurosurgeon chronicling his battle with stage IV metastatic lung cancer. It is a look at death and dying that weaves together medical and personal challenges in a moving way.

➢ Lewis, C. S. *A Grief Observed*.
Faber & Faber, 1961.

Originally published pseudonymously under the name N. W. Clerk, this is a series of sometimes raw reflections on the nature of grief following the death of Lewis's wife, Joy Davidman.

➢ Koenig, Harold G., and George W. Bowman. *Dying, Grieving, Faith, and Family: A Pastoral Care Approach*.
Routledge, 1997.

A handbook of pastoral care for end-of-life issues.

➢ Kuhl, David. *What Dying People Want: Practical Wisdom for the End of Life*.
Anchor Canada, 2003.

A series of conversations with dying people documenting what they want and need in the final days of their lives. A good primer on how to converse with the dying—and those who love them.

> Mannix, Kathryn. *With the End in Mind: Dying, Death, and Wisdom in an Age of Denial.* Little Brown Spark, 2018.

A palliative-care approach to preparation for dying and death, this book helpfully rejects many of the modern strategies of denial discussed in this book and raises questions about specifically Christian ways of speaking about death, like the last enemy and the wages of sin.

> Van Duivendyk, Tim P. *The Unwanted Gift of Grief: A Ministry Approach.* Routledge, 2006.

This guide for pastors helping people through grief encourages us to see grief as a gift, the necessary and beneficial way to come to terms with loss. A good antidote to denial strategies so common today.

Notes

1. Radical Anabaptists attempted to establish a theocracy in the city of Münster in February of 1534, after taking over the city council. Their hope was to bring in the new Jerusalem—heaven on earth. They proclaimed a society of absolute equality, polygamy, and common property and enforced such measures strictly, arousing the opposition of both Lutherans and Catholics. The city was besieged later that year and fell in June of 1535. Those leaders who did not die in skirmishes during the siege were tortured and executed afterward. The cages in which the bodies of Jan van Leiden, Bernhard Knipperdolling, and Bernhard Krechting were publicly displayed continue to hang from the steeple of St. Lambert's Church to this day. For a fuller account of this fiasco, see George H. Williams, *The Radical Reformation*, 3rd ed. (Sixteenth Century Journal Publishers, 1992), 561–82.
2. Marcus Aurelius, *Meditations IV*, 17.
3. Peters, *Sin: Radical Evil in Soul and Society* (Eerdmans, 1994).

4. Randy Stonehill, "Keep me Runnin'," track 2 on *Welcome to Paradise*, dir. Larry Norman, Solid Rock Records SRA-2002, 1975.

5. Allison Krauss & Union Station, "Everybody Wants to Go to Heaven" (Loretta Lynn, 1965), track 7 on *I Know Who Holds Tomorrow*, Rounder Records, 1994.

6. Mary Elizabeth Frye, "Immortality," Clare Harner, *The Gypsy* (December 1934).

7. This phrase was coined by N. T. Wright and is found throughout his work, especially in *Surprised by Hope*.

8. *M*A*S*H*, "The General's Practitioner," Season 5, Episode 21, dir. Alan Rafkin.

9. On the changes to MAID in general, see nationalpost.com/opinion/raymond-j-de-souza-canadians-need-more-palliative-care-not-same-day-death-on-demand. On conflict with palliative care, see nationalpost.com/pmn/news-pmn/canada-news-pmn/b-c-hospice-looking-at-legal-and-other-options-after-funding-cut-by-province. Here's a chronicle of the Christian Legal Fellowship's work on the topic: christianlegalfellowship.org/dignityforall.

10. John Paul II, *Evangelium Vitae*, Libreria Editrice Vaticana, March 25, 1995.

11. "Politics is chiefly a function of culture, at the heart of culture is morality, and at the heart of morality is religion." John Neuhaus, quoted

in Raymond Arroyo, "Father Richard John Neuhaus: A Man Animated by His Faith," *Wall Street Journal*, January 9, 2009.

12. C. S. Lewis, *The Great Divorce* (Geoffrey Bless, 1946), 75.

13. Martin Luther, "A Might Fortress is Our God," trans. Frederic Henry Hedge, text available via hymnary.org.

14. Eberhard Bethge, *Dietrich Bonhoeffer: A Biography*, rev. ed. (Fortress, 2009), 927; S. Payne Best, *The Venlo Incident* (Hutchinson, 1950), 200.

15. Luther, "A Might Fortress is Our God."

16. John Bunyan, *Pilgrim's Progress*. Accessed at utc.iath.virginia.edu/christn/chfijba6f.html. Accessed December 22, 2020.

17. See, in particular, Lewis's description of glory as "fame with God." C. S. Lewis, "The Weight of Glory," in *The Weight of Glory* (HarperOne, 2001).

18. Albert E. Brumley, "I'll Fly Away," 1929, text available via popularhymns.com.

19. Mike Bird, "Interview: N. T. Wright: The Church Continues the Revolution Jesus Started," in *Christianity Today*, October 13, 2016.

20. Thomas Hobbes, "Of the Natural Condition of Mankind as Concerning Their Felicity and Misery," in *Of Man, Being the First Part of Leviathan*, chapter XIII, The Harvard Classics, 1909–14.

21. Brumley, "I'll Fly Away."

22. Consider Luther's advice: "These books should not be held equal to holy Scripture, and yet they are good and beneficial to read"(WADB 2:547).

23. See, for example, Adolf von Harnack, *What is Christianity? Lectures Delivered in the University of Berlin during the Winter-Term 1899–1900*, esp. Lecture XI, "The Christian Religion and Its Development Into Catholicism."

24. Ludwig Wittgenstein, *Tractatus Logico-Philosophicus* 6.54.

25. For a contemporaneous account, see the first-century *Apocalypse of Zephaniah*.

26. C. S. Lewis, *The Voyage of the Dawn Treader* (Collier, 1970), 88–90.

27. Charles Wesley, "Rejoice, the Lord is King!" 1744, text available via hymnary.org.

28. See McClymond, *The Devil's Redemption: A New History and Interpretation of Christian Universalism*, 2 vols. (Baker Academic, 2018).

29. Peter Hitchens, *The Rage Against God* (Zondervan, 2010), 102–3.

30. "The Whisky Priest." *Yes Minister*. Writ. Anthony Jay and Jonathan Lynn. BBC. 2002 (1982). DVD.

31. Joseph Ratzinger, *Eschatology: Death and Eternal Life* (Ignatius, 1988), 216.

32. G. K. Chesterton, *Orthodoxy* (Harold Shaw, 1994), 10.

33. Ratzinger, *Eschatology*, 217.

34. C. S. Lewis, *The Last Battle* (Harper Trophy, 1984), 205–6.

35. John Grisham, *The Chamber*, (Doubleday, 1994).

36. David Bentley Hart, *That All Shall Be Saved*, 38.

37. Lewis, *The Last Battle*, 220.

38. Francis Ford Coppola and Mario Puzo, *The Godfather*, 1972.

39. See, for example, Martin Luther, "Preface to Latin Writings [1545]," in *LW* 34:336–37.

40. Todd Burpo and Lynn Vincent, *Heaven is for Real*, (Thomas Nelson, 2010).

41. Alex Malarkey and Kevin Malarkey, *The Boy Who Came Back from Heaven* (Tyndale House, 2010).

42. The phrase was coined by N. T. Wright and is found throughout his work, especially in *Surprised by Hope*.

43. John Updike, "Seven Stanzas at Easter" (1960), in *Telephone Poles and Other Poems* (Knopf, 1963).

44. Updike, "Seven Stanzas."

45. Thomas F. Torrance, *Space, Time and Resurrection*, xi.

46. Matthew Bridges, "Crown Him with Many Crowns," 1851, text via hymnary.org.

47. Joseph Ratzinger, *Eschatology: Death and Eternal Life* (Ignatius, 1988), 234.

48. Ratzinger, *Eschatology*, 233–38.

49. Lewis, *Last Battle*, 220.

50. John Piper, *Brothers, We Are Not Professionals* (Broadman and Holman, 2009).

51. Pat Jalland, *Death in the Victorian Family* (Oxford University Press, 1996).

52. Thomas Long and Thomas Lynch, *The Good Funeral* (Westminster John Knox, 2013).

53. Megan O'Rourke, *The Long Goodbye: A Memory of Grief* (Riverhead, 2011), 256.

54. Wesley, "Rejoice, the Lord is King!"

55. C. S. Lewis, *The Magician's Nephew* (Bodley Head, 1955).

56. J. K. Rowling, *Harry Potter and the Chamber of Secrets* (Scholastic, 1998).

57. Rowling, *Harry Potter and the Sorcerer's Stone*, (Scholastic, 1997).

58. Charles Wesley, "Jesus! The Name High over All," 1749, text via hymnary.org.

59. "The Funeral Liturgy Form II," *The Book of Alternative Services of the Anglican Church of Canada* (Anglican Book Center, 1985), 595.

60. "The Funeral Liturgy Form II," *The Book of Alternative Services*, 596.

61. See, for example, *The Sermons of the Rev. C. H. Spurgeon of London* (Sheldon, Blakeman, and Company, 1857), 177.

62. See for example George Lindbeck, *The Nature of Doctrine: Religion and Theology in a Postliberal Age* (Westminster John Knox, 1984), 118.

63. Matthew 12:20, quoting Isaiah 42:3.

64. John C. Ryle, *Light From Old Times, Or, Protestant Facts and Men*, 2nd ed. (Thynne, 1898), 165.

65. C. S. Lewis, *A Grief Observed* (Faber & Faber, 1961), 5.
66. Luther, "A Might Fortress."
67. Bob Bennett, "The Place I Am Bound," track 10 on *Songs from Bright Avenue*, prod. Jonathan David Brown, (Urgent Records, 1991) Signpost Music, 2003.

Bibliography

Austin, J. L. *How to Do Things with Words*. 2nd ed. Harvard University, 1975.

Barth, Karl. *The Word of God and the Word of Man*. Peter Smith, 1928.

Becker, Ernest. *The Denial of Death*. Free Press, 1973.

Bultmann, Rudolf. *History and Eschatology: The Gifford Lectures, 1955*. Edinburgh University, 1957.

Burpo, Todd, and Lynn Vincent. *Heaven Is for Real: A Little Boy's Astounding Story of His Trip to Heaven and Back*. Thomas Nelson, 2010.

Canadian Conference of Catholic Bishops. *Order of Christian Funerals*. Canadian Conference of Catholic Bishops/ Conférence des évêques catholiques du Canada, 1990.

Griffiths, Paul J. *Lying: An Augustinian Theology of Duplicity*. Brazos, 2004.

Grisham, John. *The Chamber: A Novel.* Doubleday, 1994.

Hart, David Bentley. *That All Shall Be Saved: Heaven, Hell and Universal Salvation.* Yale University Press, 2019.

Hitchens, Peter. *The Rage Against God: How Atheism Led Me to Faith.* Zondervan, 2010.

Jalland, Pat. *Death in the Victorian Family.* Oxford University, 1996.

LaHaye, Tim, and Jerry Walls. *Left Behind.* Tyndale, 1995.

Leithart, Peter J. *Gratitude: An Intellectual History.* Baylor, 2014.

Lewis, C. S. *The Great Divorce.* Geoffrey Bless, 1946.

Lewis, C. S. "The Weight of Glory." In *The Weight of Glory and Other Addresses.* Geoffrey Bless, 1949.

Lewis, C. S. *The Voyage of the Dawn Treader.* Harper Trophy, 1984 (1952).

Lewis, C. S. *The Last Battle.* Harper Trophy, 1984 (1956).

Lewis, C. S. *A Grief Observed*. Faber &
Faber, 1961.

Lindbeck, George. *The Nature of Doctrine:
Religion and Theology in a Postliberal Age*.
Westminster John Knox, 1984.

Lindsey, Hal, and Carole C. Carlson. *The Late
Great Planet Earth*. Zondervan, 1970.

Long, Thomas. *Accompany Them with Singing:
The Christian Funeral*. Westminster John
Knox, 2009.

Long, Thomas, and Thomas Lynch. *The Good
Funeral*. Westminster John Knox, 2013.

Lynch, Thomas. *The Undertaking: Life Studies
from the Dismal Trade*. Norton, 2009.

Malarkey, Alex, and Kevin Malarkey. *The Boy
Who Came Back from Heaven*. Tyndale,
2010.

McClymond, Michael. *The Devil's Redemption: A
New History and Interpretation of Christian
Universalism*. 2 vols. Baker Academic,
2018.

Milbank, John. *Theology and Social Theory*. 2nd
ed. Wiley-Blackwell, 2006.

Moltmann, Jürgen. *Theology of Hope*. SCM, 1967.

O'Rourke, Meghan. *The Long Goodbye: A Memory of Grief*. Riverhead, 2011.

Pannenberg, Wolfhart. *Theology and the Kingdom of God*. Westminster John Knox, 1969.

Peters, Ted. *Sin: Radical Evil in Soul and Society*. Eerdmans, 1994.

Ratzinger, Joseph. *Eschatology: Death and Eternal Life*. Ignatius, 1988.

Ratzinger, Joseph. *The Spirit of the Liturgy*. Ignatius, 2000.

Ryle, John C. *Light From Old Times, Or, Protestant Facts and Men*. 2nd ed. Thynne, 1898.

Soskice, Janet Martin. *Metaphor and Religious Language*. Clarendon, 1987.

Stott, John. *Between Two Worlds: The Challenge of Preaching Today*. Eerdmans, 1982.

Taylor, Charles. *A Secular Age*. Belknap, 2007.

Torrance, T. F. *Space, Time and Resurrection*. T&T Clark, 2000.

Updike, John. "Seven Stanzas at Easter." In *Telephone Poles and Other Poems*. Knopf, 1963.

von Balthasar, Hans Urs. *Dare We Hope That All Men Be Saved? With a Short Discourse on Hell*. 2nd ed. Ignatius Press, 2014.

Williams, George H. *The Radical Reformation*. 3rd ed. Truman State University Press, 1995.

Williams, Rowan. *The Edge of Words: God and the Habits of Language*. Bloomsbury/Continuum, 2014.

Wright, N. T. *The Resurrection of the Son of God*. Fortress, 2002.

Wright, N. T. *Surprised by Hope*. HarperOne, 2008.

Wright, N. T. *History and Eschatology: Jesus and the Promise of Natural Theology*. Baylor, 2019.

Wycliffe College at The University of Toronto, *What Does It Mean to be Human? Ghosts and Machines*. youtu.be/2IYR22ouDP8.

—

PASTORS CARE FOR A SOUL IN THE WAY A DOCTOR CARES FOR A BODY.

In a time when many churches have lost sight of the real purpose of the church, *The Care of Souls* invites a new generation of pastors to form the godly habits and practical wisdom needed to minister to the hearts and souls of those committed to their care.

"Pastoral theology at its best. Every pastor, and everyone who wants to be a pastor, should read this book."
—Timothy George, Founding Dean, Beeson Divinity School, Samford University; General Editor, Reformation Commentary on Scripture

LEXHAM PRESS

For more information, visit
LexhamPress.com/Care-of-Souls